I Think I'm Right in Saying That?

The Intellectual Chaos Continues!

Scott Robinson

ISBN 9781076511959

For my daughter
Sandy Lynn,
with all my love!

Table of Contents

Introduction *11*

Fixing the World *13*

The Social Dominator and the Authoritarian Follower *14*

Fear and Loathing in the Oval Office *16*

Libraries *18*

My First Cadaver *20*

The Ideologue *21*

Octants *22*

Our Adversary's Wildest Dreams *25*

Of Those Who Do Not Think *26*

Two Human Inventions *27*

Most People, Take 2 *28*

Friend or Foe *29*

In the Mind of the Troll *32*

Listening is Intelligence *33*

The Coming Sex Robot Market *34*

The Social Dominator Behind You *36*

Distributed Human Intelligence *38*

Saturday Morning Cartoons *42*

Unrealities *45*

The Sabertooth Strategy *49*

Hemispheres *54*

What You Would Have Me Do *60*

Moderates *62*

Hyperindividualism *63*

None of the Above *66*

The Original Humanists *69*

Clustered Hemispheres *72*

ROI *74*

The Cost of Knowledge *75*

The Factual, Objective Answer *78*

2069 *79*

In God We Trust *81*

It's Personal *84*

Diet of the Mind *88*

Money, Guns, and Dildos *92*

Relationalism *96*

Right is Left and Left is Right *98*

Generation Z *103*

Thermohaline *105*

The Truth *106*

Science and the Octants *108*

The Low-Empathy Cognitive Cluster *110*

Human Nature, Yet Again *112*

It's Not... *113*

A Good Argument *114*

On the Beach *115*

Heaven and Angels *116*

WestWingWorld *117*

The Problem *122*

Fullness of Consciousness, Bonds of Strange Loops *123*

Two Worlds *125*

Empathy and Capitalism *130*

My Partisan Friend *130*

By Accident of Birth *133*

The Digital Capitalist *134*

Universal Trust *138*

For Religion to Work... *141*

Whatever Father Says *142*

Levers of the Mind *146*

Generation Z, Part II *147*

Toxic *150*

Tipping Point *151*

Empathy, Yet Again... *152*

AI and the Self *153*

The Dangers of a Blue Wave *155*

Binkies *157*

Huddles *158*

Ideology *161*

Energy Coupons *162*

Artificial Intelligence and the US Worker *163*

On the Nature of a Book *164*

Parental *166*

Cooperation's Bad Name *169*

AI, Jesus, and Purity of Thought *170*

She Is Anyway *173*

The Opinion and the Person *174*

The Strange Loops That Are Me *175*

Men and Women *177*

Gaps *178*

Less Real *183*

Noise *184*

Immerse Yourself *185*

AI's Bad Rap *186*

Hot Nerd Talk *187*

The Selfish Group *190*

Living in the Future *192*

More Empathy *194*

The Man Without a Party *195*

Entropy, Interrrupted *198*

Man's Best EON *207*

I Was Right!!! 208

Still More Empathy *209*

Under the Sheets *210*

Generation Z, Part III *212*

Eight Chickens *215*

Nihilism *217*

The Real Problem *218*

The Savanna Principle *221*

The Robots are Coming! *223*

Choosed *228*

A Function of the Brain *229*

The Choice Was This... *230*

Hope and Fear *231*

Vectors *232*

Hello, Babies! *233*

The Suppression of Cognitive Type *238*

My ism *241*

Uncle Scott's Seven Steps *244*

Tribalism vs. Globalism *245*

Kindness is Viral *246*

If Gods There Be... *248*

Bibliography / Recommended Reading *249*

Introduction

Here we go again!

This third collection of short essays is, for me, another pride and joy – but this time around there's more going on, and that's a particularly satisfying outcome.

The usual suspects are here, to be sure: discussion of the ancient human past, the unsettling present, and the digital future; musings about the nature of mind; random echoes of joy from days gone by; and, of course, the moments of lapsed self-awareness that my gentle readers have come to expect. But there's more.

In each of these books, trial essays have come forth heralding projects in process and investigations on-going, and this one is no exception. But I'm particularly excited to cite several that I'm really excited about.

There's discussion of Jeremy England's work on dissipative adaptation, which closes the book on deitic gaps in the human narrative; Iain McGilchrist's work on the real story behind human brain hemispheres; David Brooks' 'Second Mountain' concept; and my own continuing efforts with my friend and partner Jerald Hughes in the domain of brain-based personality assessment.

Each of these informs another work in progress, making this collection a kind of sampler for things to come. It's my hope, as always, that the reader finds it both enjoyable and illuminating, and that it might smooth the way for future excursions.

Fixing the World

We don't fix the world by changing minds.

We don't fix the world by pressing our tribe's agenda (whatever your tribe might be), because no single tribe can fix the world.

We don't fix the world by reading things others post that might make us feel good about ourselves.

We fix the world in other ways, each very different from the list above.

We fix the world by considering other points of view.

We fix the world by practicing listening to other points of view.

We fix the world by defending our own points of view with something more than "I'm right, because the people who agree with me say I am!"

We fix the world through the mental exercise of having to explain why we think and feel the way we do about important matters.

We fix the world by seeing others more clearly, and understanding and clarifying our own thinking more deeply.

We fix the world by developing an appreciation of cognitive diversity, and a suspicion of echo chambers.

We fix the world by becoming more self-aware, and becoming more aware of those around us.

These things - and not the dominance of one set of opinions or viewpoints - are what will fix the world.

The Social Dominator and the Authoritarian Follower

This combination of personality types is called "the lethal union" by social psychologists. Why? Because when one of the few social dominators among us taps into a group of the many authoritarian followers among us, bad things that are normally not done suddenly become possible.

What's odd about this is that the authoritarian follower *longs* for the social dominator, needs the social dominator, will submit unquestioningly to the social dominator - while the social dominator shares *none* of the authoritarian follower's values or imperatives. It's truly a match made in hell.

The authoritarian follower is strongly, unflinchingly driven by the shared values of her/his group, committed to a specific behavioral/moral code that is so strong as to generate a belief that everyone, in the group or not, should be compelled to abide by it.

The social dominator has no moral code at all.

The authoritarian follower adores the social dominator, will refuse to see any flaw or imperfection in the social dominator, will unquestioningly obey the social dominator. It's love.

The social dominator has no love for the authoritarian follower at all.

Finally, the authoritarian follower tends to be deeply religious - not always, but nearly so - extending social hierarchy beyond the human scale, with the social dominator ascendant to some position between the follower and God.

The social dominator almost never believes in God or embraces religion, though the pretense is useful.

The authoritarian follower's identity is desperately rooted in her/his group. The social dominator needs no group to define himself.

In a nutshell, the social dominator is as opposite - in belief, motivation, world-view - of the authoritarian follower as it is possible to be. The authoritarian follower is incapable of seeing that, and the social dominator doesn't care.

Fear and Loathing in the Oval Office

It's September 2018 as this page is written, and there's much going on in Washington.

In the *New York Times*, we read the words of Anonymous, who tells of an in-house resistance to the Oval Occupant: "I work for the president, but like-minded colleagues and I have vowed to thwart parts of his agenda and his worst inclinations."

The thwarting has diverted a number of alarming, potentially catastrophic actions by the president: an impulsive assassination order; the termination of trade agreements; troop withdrawals with nuclear consequences.

And just as Anonymous speaks, veteran White House documentarian Bob Woodward reveals his new book, *Fear: Trump in the White House* (as redundant a subtitle as I've ever seen), an opus recording the words of over a hundred Trump officials and staffers that echoes the claims of Anonymous: the people surrounding the president are quietly intervening, subverting his most dangerous impulses, truncating his actions at every turn in order to prevent the worst from becoming reality.

They are, in short, acting as a kind of shadow government, in order to protect the Donald Trump from his own worst enemy. This is patently unethical, and probably illegal, and apparently mercifully effective: we have not assassinated anyone, we have not terminated trade with South Korea, nor have we withdrawn our troops there.

The actions of Anonymous and his/her in-house resistance have drawn both praise and criticism. On the one hand, at least *someone* in power is trying to keep Trump's horrific decisions contained. The GOP party leadership sure isn't. And it won't be long before we have a SCOTUS so Right-leaning that it will uphold any decree he issues.

These White House insiders weren't elected! goes the media line. *No matter how necessary their interventions, no matter the damage averted, they are acting utterly improperly!* It's hard to disagree; this is exactly the *opposite* of how the executive office should function.

No one in their right minds would *choose* for this to be our status quo.

On the other hand, the White House *itself* has become the opposite of what it should be; and so, in a Bizarro-world inversion, two negatives are yielding a positive.

No one elected these officials and staffers, it's true; and so they have no business being the check on Trump's abuses of power. The problem is, those who *were* elected, and whose sworn, Constitutional duty it is, are not lifting a finger.

Both the White House resistance and the GOP Congress do have something in common, however: a craven, deeply misaligned need to put party agenda ahead of the law, the Constitution, and the national interest - a need to advance an ideology which by its nature sweeps the principle of democracy aside whenever it's advantageous.

Libraries

It is a September Saturday morning, and my daughter has resumed her weekend dance class – and I, once again, have the happy duty of being her transportation. Our routine, over the two years she's been in this class, has been for me to pick her up and drive her to class, chatting and singing and joking as we go, then stealing away to the nearby Jeffersonville Public Library with laptop and a few reference books in my backpack for an hour of journalistic solitude.

Today, I noticed for the first time that there are administrative rooms here, free for public use, a bit quieter than the open main floor. I inquired, and was cheerfully escorted to one of these rooms, where now I sit, with my work waiting patiently in my backpack.

But I'm swelling with gratitude right now for this happy feature of our modern world, the Library - and feel I should say a few words.

My life is a progression of such buildings, and I can reconstruct who I was and how I became who I am from that progression.

Let's begin in the Garden Springs Elementary School library, where I met *Alfred Hitchcock's Three Investigators*, and the concept of the short story collection. It was here I picked up the notion that thinking could be the true action in an adventure story.

Then there was the East Point Public Library in Georgia, where I read *Andy Buckram's Tin Men*, the first science fiction I encountered, a book that assured me that young minds were capable of invention – and which I took to my grandparents' farm, where my grandfather and I began constructing a robot from tin cans.

Then came the East Union Elementary library, where I befriended Encyclopedia Brown – learning that girls were as smart as (and often tougher than) boys – and discovered *real* science fiction, in the form of *Revolt on Alpha C* by Robert Silverberg and *The Runaway Robot* by Lester del Rey. From these readings sprang my first thoughts of what human society might someday become, and how technology will increasingly reflect our humanity.

The best was yet to come. Junior high school beckoned, and I attended Darlington, an old *Hoosiers*-style pile of faded brick three stories tall (with dingy basement), high ceilings, thick oak banisters and a gym built in the Twenties – with a musty-sweet library on the third floor, where Study Hall took place: my personal heaven.

My friends and I would zip through our homework, raise our hands, and be granted grazing rights in the stacks - where I found Asimov's *I, Robot* and Heinlein's *Space Cadet* and Bradbury's *A Medicine for Melancholy* and *Something Wicked This Way Comes* – manna from heaven, all of it! - and decided to become a writer.

It was a heartbreak, but only a brief one, when I graduated to North Montgomery High, an ultra-modern building that could not have been more different – with a library that hosted Clarke's *The Nine Billion Names of God* and Bradbury's *Martian Chronicles* and a Hugo Winners collection that featured Tom Godwin's gut-wrenching "The Cold Equations" (to which I wrote a reply story, decades later).

All of that culminated at the nearby Crawfordsville Public Library, where I found *The Illustrated Man* and Asimov's *Buy Jupiter* and the novel version of *2001: A Space Odyssey* – a paperback I failed to return, and upon which there must now be a $5,000 fine, these 42 years later.

In my freelance months, when I have no office to go to, I dislike working at home. Being surrounded by my own books is a comfort, to be sure, but it's terribly lonely. I have grown accustomed to sauntering up the road to the New Albany Public Library, where I can write in peace but still be around the smiles and warmth and courtesies of other human beings – as I am this moment.

Needless to say, all of my children have subsequently had deep indoctrinations into the joys of libraries.

Libraries made me who I am.

Zeus willing, I will die in one.

My First Cadaver

I worked in a neuroscience lab in grad school, and had occasion to take a neuro class at the university's medical school (though I was not myself a medical student). At the same time, an actual doctor-in-training did a stint in our lab, to learn electroencephalography, which was the lab's central activity.

His name was David, and just for giggles he took us to the med school cadaver lab, a refrigerated room where pickled corpses were stored for examination by eager doctors-to-be.

This wasn't my first encounter with a dead person, of course – I had, at this point in life, attended many funerals – but this was the first time I actually touched one. It was named Louise (naming the cadavers is a med school tradition), and it was gray and leathery and unsettling.

I reached in and lifted a lung, examining the remains of the main circulatory conduits beneath, simultaneously fascinated and repelled, and proceeded to scrutinize the heart, then the stomach, as my colleagues watched in horror.

Finally I stepped back, proud of having found my courage in dogged intellectual pursuit.

"Traditionally," David quietly noted, "we put on gloves first…"

The Ideologue

The Ideologue is like the guy who totally bought into the Bay City Rollers and learned every last word of every single Bay City Rollers song, and he's ready and waiting to prove your band doesn't hold a candle to the Bay City Rollers – by quoting every word of a Bay City Rollers song and reading you his review of the Bay City Rollers.

The Ideologue is like the guy who only knows how to play Donkey Kong, and he plays it very well, because he plays it all the time, but when you go to the arcade with him, he will refuse to play anything but Donkey Kong, explaining that the games you enjoy are inferior to Donkey Kong.

The Ideologue's worldview is like a grade schooler's diorama, made out of stuff he dug out of his bedroom closet, modeled to look exactly like the diorama of the person who introduced him to dioramas – and if you offer him something for his diorama, he will hold it up to the diorama to see if it fits; and if it doesn't, he chucks it over his shoulder.

The Ideologue is the guy at Thanksgiving family dinner who hates turnips and red onions in his tossed salad, and thus removes all of them from the community salad bowl when it's passed around.

The Ideologue is the guy who has taken the same path home from work every day of his career – and when confronted with road work and detours gets hopelessly lost, calling home for help.

Octants

The social cognition theory (which we call 'octants', as a shorthand) that underlies many of the essays to follow is based on the parsing of political bias back in the 2006-2008 timeframe[1], when Bush II was winding down and Obama was rising. We noted patterns in political rhetoric that set us on course with text analytics, but we sought more - to understand the underlying psychology.

But it's more than psychology. As we dug into it, it's social psychology; anthropology; sociology; genetics; neuroscience. It's cross-disciplinary, so our research took years and years, even just gathering the literature together.

In a nutshell, the Octants Theory is this: that humankind survived its paleolithic infancy through intricate social cooperation, leveraging the full problem-solving potential of every individual tribe (maxing out at around 150 members total). These social structures weren't hierarchical, as we are today, but instead exercised 'situational authority' - the alpha of the moment was the man or woman most capable of solving the type of problem confronting the tribe (e.g., fighting a lion; finding shelter; figuring out where the herd went).

We recognized early on that there are several distinct cognitive types among us all, a small range of social biases in community and problem-solving that are consistent across history and literature. It occurred to us that these differences are not driven by personal choice or by social design, but are inborn - we are predisposed, genetically, to lean in the direction of one of these cognitive types. Put another way, any given population will have a distribution of people representing all the different cognitive types, and thus all the different social biases and problem-solving styles.

Several parts of the human brain are dedicated to social processing, or ancient mechanisms that feed information to social processing: the anterior cingulate cortex, which is about problem-solving; the

---

[1] My partner in this work is Dr. Jerald Hughes of the University of Texas.

insula, which is about empathy; and the amygdala, which is about fear/risk. We are all born with differing amounts of tissue in these brain regions, and thus all have different innate problem-solving capacity, empathy for others, and fear/aversion to risk. We learn, socially, how to express these things - but our 'amount' of fear, empathy, problem-solving ability, etc are with us at birth.

A final piece of this is dopamine receptivity: people with high dopamine receptivity get a subconscious Ping! signal of 'rightness' at some cognitive experience that tells them it's okay to stop reasoning and problem-solving; people with low receptivity are never happy with an answer, because that Ping! is so elusive. People who like bland music are the former; people who embrace classical music are the latter.

We found, in our studies, three axes of social response:

Egalitarian/Authoritarian social perception. Some people bias hard toward following a leader (Authoritarian); some bias hard toward group consensus (Egalitarian). These biases determine our levels of conservatism/liberalism, religiosity, etc.

Opportunity-Scanning/Threat-Scanning. Our levels of amygdala response determine how risk-taking or risk-averse we are. Some people bias hard against risk, some leap into risk. This, too, is expressed in personal behaviors and social/political opinions. Steve Jobs was an Opportunity Scanner; Bernie Sanders is a Threat Scanner, and so on.

Novelty-Seeking/Uniformity-Seeking. People who stick close to home and think things should remain as they are are Uniformity Seekers. They resist change and counsel caution in too much of it; they are exalting of tradition and our institutions. Novelty Seekers are the opposite, welcoming change and actively pursuing it. They are our inventors and writers and musicians.

We combine these axes of bias into personality types - eight altogether: EON, ETN, EOU, ETU, ATU, ATN, AOU, AON.

An ATU is a person who likely voted for Trump - Biased toward social hierarchy, uneasy with change, wishing things would remain as they have always been, wary of people unlike themselves.

An EON is a person who voted for Bill Clinton or JFK, biased toward social equality, open to change (often insistent upon it), interested in exploration and discovery.

And so on... we can think of many examples of such people in media, in politics, in history. In fact, it's quite fun to make an exercise of this.

The healthiest organizations and communities embrace a mixture of such types, as no one type can be excellent at all kinds of problem-solving; but a group that includes all types is able to solve anything. We believe that prehistory is made up of such groups, and that our modern era (sadly) makes it not only possible but easy for us to self-segregate into groups of those of our own type - diluting diversity and shutting down paths to meaningful problem-solving. (We also believe the Founding Fathers had some innate sense of this truth, and gave us a style of government that necessarily included diverse cognition as a result. We've certainly mangled that, haven't we?)

Our Adversary's Wildest Dreams

The oligarchs and despots who oppose the US are counting on a few things...

They are counting on the chaos now emanating from our highest office to distract us from their subtle presence in the on-going manipulation of Western politics;

They are counting on the cowardice of our craven, power-drunk politicians to prevent their intervention;

They are counting on the self-interest and disloyalty of our own oligarchs to keep them from standing alongside their countrymen;

They are counting on the erosion of journalistic integrity in the age of click bait;

They are counting on the dearth of critical thinking that defines ideologues of all stripe within the US electorate;

They are counting on the loud incantations of ancient stupidities to obscure their own approach;

They are counting on the illusions of privilege and birthright to separate US citizens from their true strength;

They are counting on our huddled clusters of stunted thought and perception to dilute our problem-solving power, our self-awareness, and our resolve.

The oligarchs and despots operate in the shadow of the Authoritarian - our adversary, rejection of whom brought our country into being in 1776, and against whom we stood again and again, in 1917, 1941, 1962 and now today.

Our adversary's wildest dreams are coming true.

Of Those Who Do Not Think

Many people – most people! - do not think very well. Most people are not contemplative or inquisitive; they are, in the words of *Guardian* culture critic Keith Dewhurst, "...fobbed off most of the time with utter banal rubbish."

This is true today, has always been true, and will never stop being true.

What is different today is that such people are in the spotlight, thanks to the Internet, and are broadcasting their emotions and opinions - within the context of their lack of erudition - much more loudly than before. When did we hear them in the days of broadcast television and analog radio, or print news? They had no access to those platforms.

Today, people without intellectual game have voices as loud as the best and brightest - and those of us in the center of that montage have taken to heaping scorn and disdain on them on a daily basis.

How does this ennoble us? How does this add substance and beauty to the world? Do we think for a moment that we are somehow shaming them into picking up a book, or reconsidering an ill-advised belief? What exactly do we achieve, when we demean another because they aren't shining as brightly as we perceive ourselves to be shining?

People who do not think very well do other things or equal or greater importance: they work hard, they pay their taxes; they have backyard barbecues and enjoy going to the movies and listening to music; they smile and nod at you at the grocery store; they hold the door for you at the post office. They bury their parents. They love their children.

Our scorn and disdain toward those who are not thinkers does harm on both ends of the expression. It diminishes our appreciation of humanity outside our circle, setting bridges afire and perpetuating the isolation that is poisoning us all.

We are well-advised to reconsider it, and to act accordingly.

Two Human Inventions

Two human inventions hold sway over all of human society - not only collectively, but individually.

Two human inventions utterly subvert our millions of years of evolutionary progress, the development of our brains, the emergence of our social systems. They cause our minds to short-circuit, to jump over hundreds of thousands of years of learning. They utterly subvert our identities, our behaviors, and our feelings about each other.

They have brought us - now more than ever - to the edge of self-destruction.

They are the bullet and the coin.

Most People, Take 2

Most people enjoy other people; even the most solitary and introverted among us are pleased to give others a benevolent smile and good wishes.

Most people find happiness in the joy of others, and sorrow in their sufferings; our empathy is an inborn, natural trait, shared by an overwhelming majority.

Most people are happy to share; what we call 'reciprocal altruism' is much more - it's a natural impulse to extend our own well-being to those around us.

Most people are not violent; they wish to live in peace and are relieved when others do the same.

Most people are not greedy; they don't care enough about money or possessions to go out of their way to have more than they need.

Most people love their children, and are naturally protective of children in general, sensing both overtly and innately that they are not only the future, but the best of the present.

Most people embrace kindness and decency for their own sake, and not merely as barter; it is these traits, and not bipedalism or language or opposable thumbs, that make us conscious beings.

Friend or Foe

The Human Mind is a friend to Science: beginning with the purest human minds – those of children – it is easy to see that an elemental exploration of the physical world is the most natural of impulses; and "elemental exploration of the physical world" is the very definition of science. Many rules for ensuring that these explorations lead to systematic observation and ultimately a meaningful validation have been layered into the process, but those are there to counteract our individual cognitive differences and the burdensome social barriers to knowledge we have constructed; Science remains, at its heart, those impulses of the mind to know the world, with which we all are born.

Religion is foe to Science: As Science grew strong enough to withstand the assaults of Religion, a truce emerged; Science, it was said, was one way of knowing, and Religion another, and ne'er the twain should ever meet. This truce has grown uneasy over time, as Science has revealed more and more of reality, giving us increasing solutions, as Religion has done little more than intensify our hostilities. The truth is that Religion exists to explain what the minds of men were thought incapable of grasping; but Science has made that existence unnecessary. The "gaps" in human understanding for which God has been a standby explanation are steadily being filled in by rational inquiry – and the "God of the Gaps" rules over a vanishing terrain in our knowledge and perception. The day is soon arriving when no gap remaining will be large enough for a god.

Curiosity is a friend to Science: The human being must explore the world because the human mind must know the world; as said above, the smallest child is so afflicted, imbued with a deep curiosity about all there is to see and do in the walk of life. This curiosity must be tempered with caution, as the world is indifferent to our well-being as we probe it; but the impulse will not be denied. We must venture over the next hill; we must cross the water; we must follow the sun and starts. Without this impulse, there could be no Science; it is, in fact, easy to say that Science, like Art, is the mature form of curiosity.

The Partisan is foe to Science: More than anything else, Science teaches us about ourselves – and what we have learned is more accurate and more useful than those teachings that came before. We know that we are creatures of community, having been interdependent for uncounted thousands of generations, relying on one another for survival and endurance and the joys of existence. It has also revealed to us that our strength in community is found in the differences between us, even more so than the similarities. The Partisan would not only deny the beauty and utility of these differences; he would eradicate them if he could. Science puts the lie to the Partisan's agenda, that his group and its ideas are superior, that their status is exalted; thus, the Partisan makes war on Science, despite his preordained defeat.

Socialism is a friend to Science: Science looms large among the cooperative ventures of humankind, the most cooperative species in the history of life. Across nations, across centuries, the practitioners of Science weave the tapestry of understanding that has become our protection against our own worst selves. Socialism, our most enduring survival model, is human cooperation raised up as the foundation of human community (which exists, always has and always will, as a necessary component of human persistence, despite the endless naysaying of its critics); it is the extension of the social fabric of the community of Science to the entire human enterprise, where its bread and fruit may be consumed by all, where its protection can extend to the edge of the human borders.

Capitalism is foe to Science: It was the earliest Science that gave us the keys to abundance - and with that abundance came systematic social malfeasance, the destruction of human community in favor of excess. Humankind went on to invent slavery, misogyny, bigotry, classes, and organized war, all in the name of acquisition. Capitalism has emerged in the modern world as distilled class warfare, over-rewarding the few and under-rewarding the many, justifying its existence with a grand list of tenuous rationalizations that ring in the ears of those with more. Science has put the lie to that list, one item at a time, debunking all those myths that validate the scourge of greed. Capitalism depends upon cooperation's antithesis, competition, and sets us against each other when our place in nature is to compete as one. Science knows better, and offers a safer – and ultimately more prosperous – course.

Nationalism is foe to Science: The human impulse to ascribe an explicit human exceptionalism to one's geographical tribe is unnatural, for the human brain cannot entertain a nation's worth of kin. The exercise is forlorn on every level, as there is no supporting truth to any such exceptionalism – but that is not the worst of it. The scientific worldview, free of all tribal bias, presents a portrait of intertwining physical systems, ecologies of many varieties in dynamic interaction; Nationalism is the overt configuration of an imaginary system, one that imagines itself independent of the others, physically, biologically and socially. It represents a debilitating severing of connectedness within the human species, across imagined boundary lines that sever human connectedness with most of the world.

Globalism is a friend to Science: We are a species; a species, not a nation, not a race, not a tribe. We are bound forever by our genes into one kind, more deeply and permanently joined than all our imagined discriminators and contrived categories can ever hope to unravel. We are a species, bound to one another and bound to a planet ideally suited for us – our Mother, our sustenance, our haven. The inquiries of Science are conversations with our planetary parent, our way of getting to know Her – and like so many parents, She cannot tell one of us from another. The gifts She offers back through Science, then, are without labels; they are for us all, wherever we live and thrive. We must learn to live beyond the imaginary walls and fences that separate us from one another and from so much of Her.

Science is a friend – the best friend - to Humankind: It is the ultimate tool in the building of our species; it is the ultimate weapon in our war on entropy; it is the ultimate reference in our quest to understand; it offers the ultimate healing of our inherent weaknesses; it is the ultimate refuge from our self-destructive ignorance; it is the ultimate transport into the future; it points us toward the ultimate answers to the question of who and what and why we are.

In the Mind of the Troll

Trolling. We see it all the time on the Internet: persons pretending to take an interest in a topic enter a discussion, make a few posts, zero in on this person or that, and manage to blow the original topic to pieces, reducing the participants to schoolyard antagonists, and then depart, having wreaked havoc for its own sake.

This is interesting, because in the real world, such behaviors lead to actual violence and real harm, and emotional damage at the very least - and those behaviors are not tolerated by society. Yet on the Internet, we tend to accept them as the price of doing business.

What do these behaviors reveal? What does on in the mind of the troll?

- A zero-sum view of human interaction: the troll sees the Internet as a battleground, a theater of dominance, and there can be only one winner;

- An inability to "win" through actual contribution of worthy ideas... which indicates a lack of self-esteem/confidence;

- A need to personalize the dialog: the troll starts out attacking ideas, but so strongly associates ideas with people that the attacks must settle on the people;

- Competition, not cooperation: to the troll, the former is strength, the latter is weakness.

Kinda feels like partisan politics, doesn't it?

Listening is Intelligence

Listening to the world - listening to other people - these are acts of intelligence.

These acts *define* intelligence.

We tend to associate intelligence with what we hear people say. We know a really intelligent person when we hear one, and we know a person really lacking in intelligence when we hear one.

But speaking intelligently is not itself an act of intelligence; it is a *product* of intelligence. It is an after-the-fact report of intelligent thought or behavior that has already occurred or been observed.

We can oversimplify this into an axiom: Listening is an intelligence credit; Speaking is an intelligence debit.

Put another way, the more you listen, the smarter you get; the less you speak, the smarter you really are...

The Coming Sex Robot Market

Sex robots are still quite new, but they're here to stay, it's safe to say. We see articles about them in Wired, we hear the bowels of Texas Evangelicals roaring to keep them out of Houston, we currently peek at the ad videos on Facebook. Sex robots are here, and they'll soon catch on.

We've been luridly anticipating them for decades, of course; from *The Stepford Wives* to *Battlestar Galactica* to *Westworld*, robotic bedmates have titillated our imaginations persistently. Who doesn't love the idea of a sex partner that does anything you tell them to do, exactly the way you want them to do it, whenever you tell them to?

It occurs to me, however, that there are some challenges to be overcome as sex robots make their way into the consumer mainstream. The biggest being, how will they be marketed?

We are, after all, accustomed to considerable variety in these free, media-driven times, adapted to a steady parade of options. Finding a compatible flesh-and-blood partner requires a considerable search, as we all have different tastes and preferences; would shopping for an artificial partner be any less arduous?

Well, your Uncle Scott has the answer: we can simplify the process considerably by borrowing from the marketing we see in a neighboring industry, one we're already well adapted to: automobiles!

Why not market sex robots as cars are marketed? Imagine how streamlined the process would then be! Think about it: we're all deeply acquainted with the features of automobiles, as well as the associated terms and phrases, so we have a built-in nomenclature. And there's an added bonus: there are things we just love about our cars that might be highly desirable (or at least convenient) in a sex robot! This marketing exercise could well lead to some very popular customizations.

Some terms we use to describe cars overall translate well right out of the gate (*elegant! stylish! luxurious!*), while others would only cause confusion (*family-friendly!*). Some sound good once you think about them (*sleek! sporty!*), and some are actually improvements over the sex terms they would replace (*vintage* vs. *MILF*).

Our marketing terminology gets even better when we think about features, where a sex robot function is exactly what you'd find in a car (heated seat, cruise control), but some standard features would be repurposed (airbags, rear camera). Some terms don't mean the same thing but would work well in advertising (*turbo-charged!*), and some terms would make useful technical descriptors (*fuel-efficient, power-to-weight ratio*).

In a few cases, we have to be selective; *sedan* might be technically correct (rear door), but the more modern back seat entertainment requires less thought. A few terms are obvious from the outset (*keyless entry* and *pushbutton start*), some might require a second or two of thought (*backup assist, traction control, automatic emergency braking*).

Then there are features that would appeal to specific audiences: lumbar support for older buyers, rear cross-traffic alert for those who fancy threesomes or groups.

Sex robots are also a natural fit for terms to do with usage, such as *heel-and-toe* (really good at driving stick) or *hooning* (taking her out for some high-performance pleasure). And then there are useful terms that cover both: *grip* (how well the tires hug the road) repurposes nicely: "She's got some serious grip!"

We might even suggest that designers of sex robots could take a page or two from carmakers in sheer practicality: wouldn't a 12V socket come in handy, in some scenarios? And who wouldn't love bluetooth connectivity, for hands-free calling?

And that brings us to actual sales. Can the automotive industry continue to inform us here? Will we have sex robot dealerships? Showrooms? Test drives? This seems awfully practical, and we can imagine them becoming very popular (the caveat being, there will be an aftermarket, leading to used sex robot dealerships: can you imagine the salesmen?).

The Social Dominator Behind You

I know a guy. He's good with numbers and tech and likes a creative role. He's worked all across his market and has made friends with the best of the best. He got called in to team with his old mentor and one of his favorite colleagues - another creative tech guru - to build some innovative stuff in a startup company.

This trio cranked away for months and built some amazing stuff. Behind the scenes, however, there lurked a Social Dominator.

The SD's sole objective, company mission and respective roles aside, was personal power - and this was achieved as SDs always achieve it, through emotional manipulation, false information, and exploitation.

My friend's tech guru buddy was the first to go, so repulsed by the politics and drama that he refused an astounding compensation and rank upgrade to get out. My friend's old mentor was fired, without cause, two months later.

This left my friend, alone with the innovative tech in his pocket, to deal with the SD. Who would choose such a thing?

But I told you that story to tell you this one: such behaviors will become less and less possible as the business universe rolls forward under the looming clouds of analytics and AI, and here's why:

The power of "Moneyball" (both the movie and the book) is its real-world testimony that the lesson of the Enlightenment is that human emotion cannot prevail against empirical reality. The numbers win out over human vanity, every time they are given their say; they give us a sports universe that changed overnight, morphing from an endless Oscar-style parade into a gladiatorial arena where even the Cubs can win the World Series.

This is true *everywhere* analytics and AI are creeping into the mix: the executive who surrenders decision-making to AI *will* beat his competition; the marketer who sets aside "gut feeling" for predictive analytics will score far more winning campaigns.

And the organization that cedes authority to fact and real information, management of people to performance measures over personalities, and decision-making to sober, data-driven models of yesterday, today, and tomorrow - that's the organization that will still be standing when the SD has long since peaked...

Distributed Human Intelligence

In the world of Internet technology, big changes are taking place – many of them right under our noses. Everyday devices all around us, from phones to wristwatches to clothing and even jewelry are weaving their way into the Internet, becoming givers and receivers of data that can change our lives profoundly.

This Internet of Things is growing at many times the rate of the business technology universe. The latter is the emerging repository for artificial intelligence – the ability of machines to learn and modify their behavior, so that their support of human activities is more efficient and accurate and predictive – which likewise has the ability to change the way we all live, in deep and meaningful ways.

The problem that I and others in my line of work face is a big one: how to get AI out of the clouds it's living in today, and down into the Internet of Things, where life is really happening?

The answer is something called *distributed intelligence*: the placement of machine learning down into the IoT by embedding powerful computing resources there where the action is, rather than in the corporate server room. With distributed intelligence, the devices we hold and wear and consult and live within can all begin learning from us, and the environment, and each other in real time – and offer real time responses back to us, without chasing off into the clouds.

Why is he telling us this?

I'm telling you this because the concept of distributed intelligence can be truly helpful in taking our next steps toward more fully understanding ourselves, and one another.

That said, I should disclose that I hate the *your-brain-is-like-a-computer* analogy: it is deeply misleading, and distracts from the essential truth of computing technology, that the human brain does poorly what computers do very well, and that we are a long, long way from fully understanding how to making computers that can do the things at which our brains excel.

Still, the concept of distributed intelligence not only *does* reflect important truths about how human brains work – it also throws some serious hints our way about how human brains evolved, and even how they can be improved.

Human beings, it turns out, possess distributed intelligence. What mind and consciousness each of us possesses individually is not only utterly dependent upon the intelligence of others all around us – and, for that matter, countless people who lived before we did – but we could never achieve the same mind and consciousness without it.

The arguments supporting this claim could fill books (and actually do already), but we can establish the claim around a single feature of mind: language.

Language is the basis of most of our existence as intelligent, conscious creatures. We use it to communicate with one another; to create and explicate and apply and pass on knowledge; to organize our internal models of the world, as well as the models we share with
 others; to interpret the thoughts and wisdom of those who came before; and to understand our own thoughts and memories. Without language, communication and knowledge and our own perceptions of ourselves and other people could not exist; our command of the world as apex predators would never have been achieved; and technology would never have emerged into the universe.

Here's the thing: language is the quintessential exemplar of distributed intelligence; it is, in fact, its primary moving part.

Without language, human minds can capture only a fraction of the knowledge available from others of our kind; without language, our knowledge of ourselves and others is not nearly as deep; and our ability to build on the past, as well as to enter into deep cooperation with others in the present, is virtually non-existent.

We know this for many reasons, but one of the most poignant is that there have walked among us human beings who never acquired language, and whose lives we have been able to observe closely. Language shapes the human brain, as experienced by a child learning from family and friends to speak at a very early age, and the shape of such a brain is required for all the knowledge and consciousness we experience by default. Without it, our relationships are shallower; our potential, sharply truncated; our self-awareness, less rich and nuanced.

Victor, the Wild Child of Aveyron, is one of several examples. Found in the woods at around age 12 outside a French village two centuries ago, he had lived on his own in the wild and never learned to speak. And despite his health and anatomical uniformity, was unable to learn how.

He was able to form limited bonds with others – the teacher who studied him, a woman who looked after him – but kept trying to run away, to flee civilization and return to the woods. He died young.

Victor lacked what Douglas Hofstadter calls *strange loops* – the bits and pieces of others, their thoughts and emotions and the substance of experiences shared with them – that we incorporate into our own thoughts, the consciousness that forms in human beings due to the community we experience from birth to death. Put another way, Victor's brain – and thus his mind and consciousness – lacked the ingredients that we take for granted, those ideas and concepts and facts and truths that build a rich world within us.

Language throws open those doors of shared experience, acting as a supercharger that causes our minds and awareness and consciousness to be amplified many times over. There are other contributing factors – our genetic diversity, the dangers of the world that cause us to innovate, and an environment in perpetual change – and they have all combined to make us something far greater, in sum, than we could ever hope to be alone.

We are taught by our culture, which is tilted precariously toward a false notion of individuality that has no real basis in reality, that we are autonomous creatures – that we can be self-sufficient, relying on no one else, solitary successes whose reason for being is to be better than those around us. That's not even close to true; we are, each of us, far stronger and smarter and more capable because we are part of a greater whole than we could possibly be on our own.

The human story is about to improve in giant leaps, because of the new tools we are now creating. We are about to begin healing from the crippling missteps of the past 10,000 years. Part of that story involves one of those new tools – distributed intelligence. But it is just a reflection of a tool we've possessed far longer, one that given us deep gifts, a generator of miracles, now embedded in our DNA: distributed human intelligence, our legacy, our substance, our future.

Saturday Morning Cartoons

I am an early riser. It is not unusual for me to be out of bed before 7am on a Saturday morning, ready to write in the quiet of a house still asleep.

But recently I was visiting family on a Saturday morning and there was a youngster up and out of bed before me, watching TV – and it wasn't a school morning. No reason he couldn't have slept in!

Except there was a reason.

Half a century ago, I was the kid who was up at 7am on a Saturday morning. I was the kid who slipped out of bed, trying to not wake my little brother, tip-toeing to the kitchen to fix myself some Cocoa Puffs and make my way to the family room.

See, in our house, whoever got to the TV first on Saturday morning commanded that TV until Mom and Dad got up and implemented turn-taking. And back then, Saturday morning was the only time of the week that cartoons were available on TV.

That is, of course, hard to convey to the modern youngster, who has at their command more than one 24/7 cartoon channel. Nor is it unusual for the average US household to have more televisions in the house than children (the RV in the driveway at this family gathering has three all by itself).

But back then, in the early Seventies, there were no 24/7 channels of any kind. There were only four channels altogether – the three broadcast networks and public television. And few homes had more than one TV set.

So it was first come, first serve at the Robinson household on Saturday morning.

It's difficult to describe that thrill to a contemporary child. It's difficult to frame having to choose between the cartoon on CBS and the one on NBC, since DVR (or even video tape recording) did not yet exist.

It's difficult to explain that this wonderful window of celluloid celebration lasted a mere four hours, giving way after lunchtime to old movies and cooking shows and ABC's *Wide World of Sports*. Tough choices had to be made; turf had to be defended. Attention to the unfolding laughs and adventures on the small screen had to be fortified against a gradually stirring household and the emerging cacophony of younger siblings.

This was another time, another era, another age; it had its own feel, a signature, an identity – a unique sensibility. There had never been a time like it, and the excesses to follow erased, in the end, all that made it special.

It was the time of *Scooby-Doo, Where Are You?*, the first of many cartoons to feature the empirical super-sleuths Fred and Daphne and Velma and Shaggy and their mangey, cowardly, lovable mutt – a show vastly superior to its sequels, *The New Scooby Doo Movies* and *Scooby Doo and Scrappy Doo* and *A Pup Named Scooby Doo* and *Shaggy & Scooby Doo Get a Clue*.

It was the time of the Road Runner and the Coyote – the same joke over and over – and over, and over, and over – which, like "Who's on First?", never ever stops being funny.

It was the time of the *Wacky Races*, with Penelope Pitstop and Peter Perfect and Rufus Ruffcut and the Bulletproof Bomb and the Bouldermobile and those ruffians, Dick Dastardly and Muttley and their Mean Machine.

And, of course, *Archie* and his Riverdale pals, Jughead and Betty and Reggie and Veronica and Moose and Dilton, and their spin-offs, *Josie and the Pussycats* and *Sabrina, the Teenage Witch* – all of which live on today in live action incarnations.

Speaking of live action cartoons, the early Seventies served those up as one of its great innovations – with young Billy Batson and his Mentor traveling the highways and by-ways of America, shouting *Shazam!* in times of dire need... a thrill that we have relived in movie theaters this very season. And *Mighty Isis* and *H.R. Pufnstuf* and *Lancelot Link, Secret Chimp* and the superb *Land of the Lost*.

There were real TV thrills brought down to cartoon (*Star Trek*) and real people, as well (the *Harlem Globetrotters*). There was avante garde (*Make a Wish*, a stream-of-consciousness exercise for children hosted by Harry Chapin's little brother Tom), movie characters in the spotlight (*The Pink Panther*), bona fide adventure (*Jonny Quest*), and sci-fi on the coattails of *Star Wars* (*Space Academy, Jason of Star Command*). Superheroes abounded, from Superman and Batman and Aquaman and the Justice League to Spider-man and Captain America and the Mighty Thor (and lamer incarnations like *Superfriends*).

And all of this was somehow not only legitimized but immortalized by the ultimate Saturday morning innovation, *Schoolhouse Rock* – with its "Conjunction Junction" and "Three is a Magic Number" and "I'm Just a Bill" and "Zero, My Hero" and "Interjections!" and "Figure Eight" and "Interplanet Janet" - all of which taught us more than we ever learned in school. *Schoolhouse Rock* inexplicably ennobled all the rest of it; if we didn't feel special before, we certainly did once those delectable three-minute bursts of knowledge came on the scene.

The end of the era came slowly. NBC abandoned Saturday mornings in 1992, and CBS soon followed. ABC held out as long as it could, all the way to 2004. And the CW, a second-tier network with treats like *Sonic X* and *Digimon Fusion*, caved in 2014, when the FCC imposed a three-hour educational TV requirement – and CW, like many other networks, decided it was better to give Saturday mornings over for that, rather than prime time.

It's difficult – nay, impossible – to convey the wonder of that era to the youngster on the couch today, whose world is packed with riches he takes completely for granted, for whom this morning is just like any other. It's impossible to get past the I-walked-two-hours-through-snowstorms-to-get-to-school nostalgia of my experience, when Saturday morning cartoons were sparse treasures, like prizes in cereal boxes. I understand that the youngster on the couch is perfectly happy as he sits there, soaring with today's *Teen Titans*...

...but I still feel like the lucky one.

Unrealities

It's stylish these days to look at Donald Trump, tracts of Congress, political parties, this religious group or that, any particular tribe that seems far off on some tangent, and describe them as lost in an alternate reality.

So prevalent is this phenomenon that the media today describes the political polarization in the US in exactly those terms: liberals and conservatives are now said to live in completely separate realities.

This is not hyperbole; it is easily observable, day to day. When Trump can speak off the top of his head about national security, contradicting his own intelligence officials, and the Right sees a powerful leader, far wiser than all the nation's top experts combined, while the Left sees an impulsive nincompoop preening for attention - 'reality' is most certainly off on a long vacation.

We can look at climate change deniers, Flat Earthers, Young Earth Creationists, apocalyptic Dominionists, moon landing deniers, and any number of other such tribes and say much the same thing: these people have built their own version of reality, moved in, and locked the door behind them.

We could leave it at that, but we won't. If we look at such people and dismiss them as having a troubled relationship with the truth, we're in a troubled relationship with the truth ourselves. And, truth to tell, we're all in trouble anyway.

Any honest assessment of the more extreme unreality denizens must necessarily include a scrutiny and understanding of the unreality itself – where do these bubbles of fictitious living originate, and how do human minds accommodate them? The answer isn't ideological; it isn't even really social, at least not completely – it's neurological.

The social brain is the product of thousands of generations of protein surplus, shared experience in lifelong tribal survival, and genetic fortune: there is tissue in the human skull purposed for modeling the world – for building out a personal, local understanding of the environment and those with whom it is shared. This model is the place where all of our thoughts and ideas are born, as well as the destination of our emotions (which originate in deeper areas of the brain). It's the place where realizations occur, actions are contemplated, behaviors organized, and perceptions of others processed. It's where our past meets the present, and where our future is anticipated; it's where the physicality of rocks and trees and stream and sky meet up with eating, sleeping, hunting, exploring, and living.

In short, it's the personal reality bubble generator that resides inside us all. It's the core of what enables human existence as we experience it.

We all build a personal reality bubble from the moment of birth. That bubble contains a great deal: a map of our local world, including the home we are raised in, the stores we shop in, the schools we attend, the park we play in; it includes our families, our friends, our neighbors, and the glimpses of the world beyond that trickle in from television and newspapers (and, today, the Internet). Consulting this model that lives within our minds is how we are able to understand the things that happen to us each day, how we perceive others, plan our activities, understand ourselves, our behaviors with others, our reflection on the past and our anticipation of the future.

This almost magical ability evolved over several million years. And it served us just fine – until lately.

Today (and for thousands of years now) it's possible to build world models inside our heads that bear only the most superficial resemblance to the real thing. We have the ability to fashion alternate realities, fine-tune them, believe in them utterly, and share them with others. We can construct consensual hallucinations, invest our existence in them, and remain within them our entire lives.

How can this be? It's a result of our ability, unmatched among all creatures, to share information, to inform our own experience by adding to our world models the knowledge and experiences of others. This ability, an astounding survival tool throughout our evolution, is suddenly as much a liability as a strength.

We have the ability to construct worlds within our heads that veer wildly from reality, because we embrace information about it, provided by others, that isn't true; our power to absorb their knowledge and experience, evolved to enhance our understanding of the world (and of them), is now not only potentially a failed path to understanding, but one to explicit *mis*understanding.

Worse, our experience of others – the exercise of the deepest bonds possible between living, breathing beings – can now be utterly false; we can look at another of our kind and believe that person to be someone they utterly are not, either by the report of others or our own mis-filtered perceptions. We can not only fail to know and understand another person – we can become utterly convinced that they are someone they are not.

And worst of all, this capacity for the building of false world models is not only prevalent, it is indulged in constantly and with both indifference and malice; our inner lives have been commoditized, rigged to suit the needs of those who can profit through our misunderstanding of the world, of others, and of ourselves.

No one is exempt. Each of us, to some degree, hosts a model of the world that is in some ways false, contrived, or fantasized – some more than others, of course, but it just isn't possible to live in the modern world without some amount of this inner-world corruption.

Where did we go wrong?

It's hard to say, exactly – but I'd put my money on the invention of spoken language.

We existed in close-knit, productive, skilled tribes for thousands of generations before we gained the knack of encoding our verbal noises to carry meaning. Prior to that time, per epidemiologist Donna Armstrong, we had long since mastered the art of reading meaning in the faces and body language of our peers; we could learn more from eye contact, in our distant past, than we learn today through lengthy conversation.

Imagine living in that distant past, building a model of the world in one's mind, mapping the landscape and the sky and all that it contained, knowing all of one's extended family, and having that information be a false reality. Imagine holding false ideas about the behaviors of predators, the dangers of threatening weather, the edibility of flora, and the traits and motivations of everyone around.

Imagine, in a nutshell, surviving in the distant past in a bubble of unreality like the ones we live in now.

I don't think any Cro-Magnon citizen, so entranced, would last long at all.

Technology has removed most of the danger from the modern world, essentially giving us the luxury of living exclusively in our fake-world bubbles. That doesn't make the unreal world in our heads any less destructive – just less immediately dangerous.

Religions do it. Political parties do it. Advertisers do it. Pop culture does it. All of our social structure, our socioeconomic classes and our institutions, our educational systems and our civic infrastructure rely upon these fake models, these rigged unrealities that are constantly crafted and nurtured in our heads. Most of the information we take in – formally, casually, incidentally, and even for entertainment – is sculpted to nudge us into believing the world is something it isn't, and to massaging our emotions to be on board with the illusion. Fox News, of course, has raised this to an art form.

Isn't that disheartening? Isn't it even more than a little frightening?

The tragedy of it is that it need not be. From birth to death, we retain all of our original firmware, the programming imbued by nature for sensing and perceiving and discovering the world, and building out a version of it in our minds. It's written deep in our nervous systems; we couldn't stop if we tried.

All it takes, to bring our world within into harmony with the world without, is the decision to become aware of what's going into that world within, to scrutinize it and rigorously test it, holding on to only those fragments we can safely judge to be authentic.

And all that decision requires, to become reality – to bring us back to reality – is time. And determination.

The Sabertooth Strategy

Cold shadow broke the dry veil of silence that enshrouded the vast, burning veldt outside. A faraway water-drip echoed through the cool darkness; stale heat roiled out of the gargantuan feline's hot, damp fur into the algid air. With a throaty growl, the Sabertooth announced his presence as the thick pads of his paws *thapped* against the gray rock floor of the cave.

A pair of green eyes blinked into being in the blackness beyond; the Hyena emerged in utter soundlessness, drooling malevolently, his black coat smelling of death. He nodded conspiratorially.

Behind them, the Lion slid into the cavern with an agitated shudder of his sweaty mane, impatiently completing the sinister triumvirate.

"Well," said the Sabertooth, "This shit has gone on too goddamn long."

"Tell me about it," agreed the Lion, nodding over his left shoulder at a barely-healed tear in his gluteus medius. "They damn near nailed me last week out at Big Rock. It's those fucking obsidian spear tips. They're sharp as hell and they hurt like a sonofabitch."

"The spears are bad enough," the Sabertooth opined, "but the real danger is that they're starting to get their shit together. They're *organized*."

"Yes!" hissed the Hyena. "Organized! They surround us, and the odds change. One-on-one, they are delectable; six-to-one, we're fucked."

The Lion nodded wryly. "True dat."

The Sabertooth paced. "Any one of them against any one of us, they end up shitting themselves and running, and *BOOM!* Pass the ketchup! But when they're in a group-"

"- they're coordinated," the Hyena frowned. "It's uncanny! It's as if they're... *organized*."

"Exactly," the Sabertooth nodded ruefully. "When they surround you, the whole intimidation thing just tanks. When you're facing down three of them, you're waving your ass like a dartboard at the other three."

"Tell me about it," said the Lion.

"What is there to do?" the Hyena groused. "They outnumber us a hundred to one!"

The Sabertooth paused in his pacing. "It's not just getting tagged with the spears," he muttered. "I don't know about you guys, but I miss the days of three square meals a day."

"This is true," the Lion nodded. "Since they've gotten 'organized,' we haven't eaten nearly as well."

"I used to pick them off just for fun sometimes, even when I wasn't particularly peckish," the Hyena agreed. "Kept me limber."

"Not trying any of that shit now," the Lion lamented.

"We're agreed that this is an unacceptable situation," the Sabertooth noted with furrowed brow. "We need to take action. Here's what I'm thinking, boys."

He settled on his back haunches and took a deep breath.

"Question: what's the difference between how things are now and how things used to be?"

The Lion blinked. "Well, they know that if they form a circle around us, they can kill us or at least wound us. We can only pick them off one-on-one."

"True, but that's not what I'm getting at: they used to keep an eye out for us, because they were scared shitless; but now they're constantly on their guard and willing to take us on – because they know how to win."

"Well, there are always stragglers and the occasional dimwit foraging alone," the Hyena pointed out. "Otherwise we'd all have starved by now."

"That's true," the Sabertooth agreed, "but that scenario robs us of control; we are at the mercy of random chance, and I for one find that completely unacceptable."

"I hear ya," said the Lion.

"We need to regain the upper hand, and I have an idea how that can work."

The Hyena and Lion stared expectantly. The Sabertooth rose up off his back haunches.

"Misdirection," he explained. "As things stand now, their social organization is based on cooperation and unity; they are systematically on the watch for us, and primed for aggression."

"Yeah," the Hyena shrugged, "So?"

"So, let's give them something new to be wary of," the Sabertooth continued, "a new target for their aggression: each other!"

The other two were silent, absorbing this weighty thought.

"If they're more afraid of each other than they are of us, their guard will be down, and we can pick them off as we please, and they will hardly even notice us."

The Lion shook his head. "How are you going to get them to all turn on each other? They're a social species; everyone for himself is our style, not theirs. They've been living in big tribes for thousands of generations."

"I'm not talking about every man for himself," the Sabertooth elaborated. "I'm talking about dividing them; two groups, and set one group against the other."

The Lion was confused; the Hyena was beginning to nod comprehendingly.

"So," he mused, "instead of being constantly ready to attack us, each group would be constantly ready to attack the other."

"I'm afraid I'm still not seeing it," the Lion frowned. "What could possibly shake their unity? Cooperation has raised their standard of living considerably."

The Sabertooth grinned, which was quite a frightening image. "These are not bright folks," he replied. "They only seem smart when they act in concert. Each one of them is just following everyone else; as individuals, they don't know very much and don't think very well. They're too dependent on the group for behavioral cues. They aren't self-aware enough to realize that they're very inexperienced at thinking independently."

"-whereas we do it all the time," the Lion nodded, "which gives us the advantage. I think I see where you're headed here. But I still see problems."

"Tell me your concerns."

"To divide them," the Lion said, "won't you need some wedge issue, something divisive enough to trigger this shift in attention and aggression?"

The Sabertooth chortled. "These maroons? Nah! They're as vain as they are stupid. Appealing to the vanity of individuals will upset the unity of the group."

The Hyena nodded. "I can see it," he said, "but we still need a strategy."

"Here's what I've come up with," the Sabertooth continued. "Next time you catch one of them unawares, don't eat them…"

"Why the hell not?"

"Hear me out. Don't let them *all* go, everyone's gotta eat, but the idea is that we catch-and-release for a while – and the ones we don't eat, we schmooze.

"We tell them not to worry, we've gone on a new diet; they eat gazelle, we tell them that we, too, are strictly gazelle, now. Tell them it's a carb thing, whatever. Fake news! Then we lay on a little gaslighting: convince the curly-haired ones that the straight-haired ones are conspiring to overturn tribal mating policy along partisan lines, and vice versa."

"What partisan lines?" the Lion asked. "They don't have any partisan divisions."

"Exactly. We *create* a partisan division."

"Over curly hair and straight hair?"

"Why not? What does it matter? Like I said, they're vain and they're stupid; find *anything* we can that makes them believe some of them are better than others, and I'm telling ya, we're home free: they'll start fighting each other, and we can feast on them as we please and they'll never know it."

The Lion pondered this thoughtfully, then nodded. "It could work, yes."

The Hyena grinned savagely. "I like it."

"We're agreed, then?" the Sabertooth asked. "Then let's spread the word to the other megafauna. Catch-and-release! Vain-and-stupid! We'll have them spearing each other like river trout in no time."

The Lion roared. The Hyena howled.

The Sabertooth turned and bounded out of the cave.

"C'mon, boys," he cried out happily, "let's party!!!"

Hemispheres

What features of our brains determine our social and political views and behaviors?

As it turns out, one of the most important is found between the hemispheres of the brain.

We've all heard the Left Brain, Right Brain arguments in the past - clichés from a generation ago, nurtured by pop culture, that tell us "left-brained" people are logical and verbal, while "right-brained" people are emotional and creative. Many of us have been exposed to this concept so often that we've just assumed it to be true.
The truth is far more complicated.

The expert in this area is British psychiatrist Iain McGilchrist, who has studied the actual neurophysiological divide between the left and right hemispheres of the brain through his own patients and the growing literature on the subject - in particular, those differences we see in perception, cognition, emotion and behavior when one hemisphere or the other is damaged.

He has articulated these fascinating differences in countless presentations, talks and interviews, and his own book *The Master and the Emissary*. He is quoted below in the Hidden Brain podcast with host Shankar Vedantam, from February 2019.

"In motor terms, it's fairly straightforward that the left hemisphere controls the right side of the body and receives messages from it and vice versa," he said. "But in terms of psychological life, they have quite different kinds of roles. They have quite different dispositions. And I believe evolutionarily, they are - if you like - addressing different questions."

Asymmetrical

First among McGilchrist's assertions is that it is an empirical certainty that the human brain's hemispheres are asymmetrical - that is, when one side is damaged, certain behaviors and deficits will emerge in the shift to dependency upon the other, and that these will differ considerably and consistently, depending on whether the damage is on the left or right.

Moreover, this asymmetry is present not only in human beings but in all mammals. For that matter, it's present in all creatures great and small - in anything that has a neural network, from reptiles to worms. And the natural question is, Why?

The answer, he said, because the old Left-Right dichotomy is wrong: the brain's two sides don't divvy up tasks into Reason Here, Emotion There; it's because the two sides of the brain do the same things differently.

The reason all creatures have a divided brain is so that they can have two different versions of reality at their disposal. Every living creature has two urgent tasks: 1) eat, and 2) avoid being eaten. The left hemisphere focuses on the first, the right on the second. We must have both, and they must co-exist and function simultaneously for obvious reasons: if we do one to the exclusion of the other, we either don't eat or we get eaten.

Details, details

The left hemisphere is focused on the task at hand - getting food, more often than not. It is the bird going for the worm; it is the lion pouncing on the gazelle; it is the chimp plucking a berry from a bush. The left hemisphere lives in the moment, accomplishing the job in progress.

Other examples were presented in the Hidden Brain broadcast: the left hemisphere is where the musician turns when rehearsing a trouble passage in a piano piece, practicing fingering; it is the basketball player dribbling the ball and shooting it.

The right hemisphere's task follows: for the musician, it is integrating the rehearsed passage into a full performance; it is the basketball player's awareness, while dribbling or shooting, of where all the other players are.

In the wild, while the left hemisphere is providing attention and focus on acquiring food, the right hemisphere is providing cover, maintaining global awareness of the surroundings, remembering the moments before and anticipating the moments to come.

Simplifying a not-so-simple idea, the difference boils down to this: "The right hemisphere takes in the whole at the start," McGilchrist explained. "The left hemisphere unpacks that and enriches it. But then that work being done, it needs to be taken back into the whole picture, which only the right hemisphere can do."

Both are functioning in the same place at the same time. But they are profoundly distinct: they essentially provide two different accounts of reality.

Left Meaning, Right Meaning

Nuance begins to emerge when we consider the subtleties introduced by hemispheric differences in human communication. McGilchrist points out that it's the left brain's job to perform literal interpretation; it's the right brain's job to pick up tone, implication, insinuation - not the meaning of a word, but the emotions conveyed in the way it is spoken. The left brain picks up only explicit meaning; the right brain picks up shadings in how it is conveyed.

For this reason, metaphor is particularly tricky for the left brain. "As some philosophers have pointed out, metaphor is how we understand everything," he said. "And they point out that, actually, particularly scientific and philosophical understanding is mediated by metaphors. In other words, the only way we can understand something is in terms of something else that we think we already understand. And it's making the analogy, which is what a metaphor does, that enables us to go, 'I see, I get it.'

"Now, if you think that metaphor is just one of those dispensable decorations that you could add to meaning - it's kind of nice, but probably a distraction from the real meaning - you've got it upside down," he continued. "Because if you don't understand the metaphor, you haven't understood the meaning. Literal meaning, however, is a peripheral, diminished version of the richness of metaphorical understanding. And what we know is the right hemisphere understands those implicit meanings, those connections of meanings, what we call connotations, as well as just denotations.

It understands imagery. It understands humor. It understands all of that."

Time

The left hemisphere, McGilchrist continued, is "very goal-driven, but very short-term goal-driven. It wants to grasp things that are within reach...so it has a very direct, linear idea of a target and let's go and get it."

"The left hemisphere can't deal with anything that is moving," he went on. "It fixes things. It likes things to be fixed because then you can grab them. You can't grasp your prey, you can't pick up something unless you can at least immobilize it for that second while you're interacting with it."

The right hemisphere, on the other hand, likes flow; time is a river on the right, constantly in motion.

Values

The two sides even have differing values. The immediacy and craving for the concrete, the graspable, make the left brain's concept of values very mechanical, algorithmic, while the right brain's take on values is more holistic.

"If you disable, temporarily, the right temporoparietal junction - which you can do with a painless procedure - and ask people to solve moral problems, they give quite bizarre answers to them based on an entirely utilitarian understanding of them.

"An example is, a woman is having coffee with her friend. She puts what she thinks is sugar in her friend's coffee, but it's in fact poison, and the friend dies. Scenario two, a woman is having coffee with her friend whom she hates, she wants to poison her - and she puts what she thinks is poison in the coffee, but it's sugar, and the friend lives. Which is the morally worse scenario?

"Now, all of us using our intact brains say, well, the one in which she intended to kill her friend. But no, if you disable the right hemisphere, the good old left hemisphere says, well, obviously the one in which she died. The consequence is what matters. So values are not well-appreciated, I think, by the left hemisphere."

Aware and Not

Finally, there's the question of how the two sides of the brain see each other.

Not surprisingly, as the guardian of the big picture, the right hemisphere is aware of the left, and can monitor what it is doing - that's the right hemisphere's job. The left hemisphere, on the other hand, is tasked with immediate tasks; it must maintain a narrow focus, and has no bandwidth or need for awareness of the right hemisphere. It believes that what is sees is all there is.

McGilchrist told the story of a physician and patient who had experienced right hemisphere damage. She had the odd belief that her arm did not belong to her, but that she had found it in her bed.

"What we're seeing here is a phenomenon called denial, which is a feature of the way the left hemisphere works," he said. "So if you have a left hemisphere stroke, so your right hemisphere is still functioning, you're very aware of what deficits you have. If you have a right hemisphere stroke, you are completely unaware of there being anything wrong. So if you have a paralyzed left arm, which is often a consequence of a right hemisphere stroke, more often than not you will deny that there's any problem with it. If asked to move it, you will say there, but it didn't move.

"If, on the other hand, I bring it in front of you and say, 'Whose arm is this, can you move it?', they say, 'Oh, that's not mine. That belongs to you, doctor, or to the patient in the next bed'... They're simply incapable of understanding that there is something wrong here that involves them."

The left brain's focus is on body parts; the right brain focuses on awareness of the body as a whole.

Emotional divide

Another difference between brain hemispheres is how emotions lateralize between them.

The big-picture orientation of the right brain makes it the center of understanding of other peoples' emotions, as they are part of that big picture. "Broadly speaking," per McGilchrist, "the right hemisphere is more emotionally literate." It is where understanding of the point of view of others emerges, and likewise enables a greater range of expression. When opposition presents itself, the impulse of the right brain is to understand and cooperate, which serves the big picture.

The intense in-the-moment focus of the left brain, on the other hand, renders it dismissive of external emotions, and self-defensively prone to anger when interrupted, which understandably serves its purpose. When opposition presents itself, the impulse of the left brain is to obstruct and repel, which serves the success of the immediate task.

We are left with a complicated but compelling portrait of how our brains move us through the world and through our lives, once McGilchrist's portrait of the hemispheres has been thoroughly reviewed. It's easy to see how the pieces fit together, how their cooperation has kept us alive and thriving and - perhaps most importantly - that we can't manage without both.

What You Would Have Me Do

Among my many friends are those whose frame of world require more than I will give - and thus we stand apart.

My Conservative Friend would have me surrender my will and judgment to the group; to accept ideology as my guide, to say nothing of leaders selected according to criteria that have little to do with leadership; he would have me fear those I shouldn't, view Science with suspicion, and accept as superior those more powerful than I. He would have me treat all beyond the tribe as suspect, and join the chorus of anger that paints all outsiders as enemies. And, of course, embrace a moral frame that feels, to me, shallow and disingenuous.

My Liberal Friend would grant me my embrace of Science and Reason, but only when convenient - and that, to me, is unacceptable; s/he would have me treat Others with a default of deference and respect and acceptance - as long as they aren't Conservatives. S/he would have me chant the mantra of inclusiveness - as long as I shut out those who do not chant with me. And, of course, s/he would have me dial down the fear (not a bad thing in itself) to the point where I would fail to see those dangers sitting right next to me.

My Libertarian Friend would throw his arms wide open, welcoming me, vicariously, into my own private community of one; he would have me close down that part of me that roams the earth with brothers and sisters by my side, to silence my trust that we are stronger standing together, rather than apart; he would have me calmly accept the more tragic fates of those around me - and, of course, to take up the lie of autonomy, which Science and Reason have long since called out.

I love each of you, my friends, but this I know: I am less than I can be, less than I should be, when I step into any of your circles. Whatever bleats persist in my heart, they are distracting *dings* that must yield to the calm and unemotional truth that I am stronger, better, more moral, more just, more honest, and more wise when I stand apart from your collectives, and create my own collective (which includes you all) – a collective that must necessarily be boundary-free.

The signals in my brain strongly urge me to dwell among those whose thoughts resemble mine, as you do; but Nature crafted a better plan, a diversity of thought and feeling that empowers us all when we embrace it, over and above the comfort of convenient mirrors.

And so I will join none of your groups. I will, instead, continue to accept and embrace you all - despite the fact that I will never do those things that you would have me do...

Moderates

The Right has spent 25 years purging itself of moderates. Today the GOP is damn near moderate-free. But I am disturbed to note that the Left seems to be mirroring this troubling trend, expressing disdain for centrist attitudes among its own.

This is what makes us strong as a nation - and, frankly, as a species - is the acceptance and even celebration of our diverse perspectives.

A moderate is, by definition, an agent of compromise; they do not need to "win" at all costs.

A moderate is accepting of incremental change; in the moderate's world, there is no other kind.

A moderate is, by inclination, a negotiator; none of the moderate's wants are on the table in a partisan contest, so dealing favorably and effectively with those to either side is really the moderate's only path to satisfactory outcomes.

A moderate naturally possesses greater immunity to the emotional siren song of the amygdala, which calls for combat, and dopamine, which begs for satiation; this keeps the moderate in the game for the entire nine innings, where partisans and ideologues bail more easily.

A moderate is more inclined to apply critical thought, because s/he must process more external points of view.

Lacking the social cohesion of a home tribe, the moderate will make the greater effort to get along with everyone, and go the extra mile to hear and understand those of differing viewpoint.

It's easy to understand and respond to those viewpoints that crowd the rails, but those that don't are no less essential: we need thinkers who can easily occupy the middle ground and see clearly in every direction.

In fact, we may never have needed them more than we do right now.

Hyperindividualism

Once upon a time, David Brooks was a soldier of the conservative right.

During this period, he had wandered out of a liberal youth (because he "came to his senses") and across the moderate plains to become a semi-incendiary gadfly in the pre-Tea Party days, arrogant and cavalier and none too concerned with the moral implications of his party's demeaning and misleading rhetoric. The farther he wandered, the more he reflected his chosen tribe's increasingly tenuous connections to truth and reality.

There came a moment when a switch flipped inside David Brooks's head, and he began to see a bigger picture. He turned from the conservative path - or, at least, the precarious path of his peers - and set out in a new direction, pursuing a more honest odyssey.

It cost him dearly in standing with those peers, but he would not be deflected. His new journey was one of discovery, revelation, and - perhaps most significantly - humility. David Brooks sought to rediscover who he was, and in the process, he came to view the people around him in new ways.

In a series of books - *The Social Animal, The Road to Character* - he explored fresh approaches to understanding others, and thereby came to understand himself and the society around us all very differently.

His latest work, as of this writing, is called *The Second Mountain*, and it frames Western society as it is in this moment, alongside the better society we have been in the past and need to become again.

The quest society lays before us, he writes, is the climbing of a mountain - a quest in pursuit of self and gratification. But there is a second mountain, Brooks asserts, one of rediscovery of our connections to the world, the society that enables us, and the people around us.

It's worth our time to survey both mountains.

The first mountain has a path called *hyperindividualism*, a social frame that is centered on the person, rather than the group. Brooks notes that this path has widened considerably since the post-war years, as technology and consumerism have blossomed in the showers of Western wealth.

The messages of hyperindividualism are many, Brooks notes, listing them all:

- Life's journey is individual and personal, and the goal should be to reject the interests of collective humanity in favor of personal happiness;

- That happiness is accomplished through achievement, success, the accumulation of wealth and power and status;

- The essence of fulfillment is being better than others, and that betterment follows the shedding of restraints imposed by society;

- Self-sufficiency, self-actualization and autonomy are the noblest of goals.

This is the plan of action suggested by the society we inhabit on every channel, at every level, Brooks notes. Our economy, our culture, and our politics all derive from this principle of hyperindividualism. It is the book of axioms that defines the lives of millions in his own Baby Boomer generation and the X that followed.

But hyperindividualism, Brooks insists, is a lie. Hyperindividualism is toxic.

Hyperindividualism "gradually undermines any connection not based on individual choice," he writes, "the connections to family, neighborhood, culture, nation, and the common good. Hyperindividualism erodes our obligations and responsibilities to others and our kind."

That erosion, he continues, has created a long list of problems: social isolation, polarization, the weakening of the family as a social structure, tribalism, a general loss of community, and "a spiritual crisis caused by a loss of common purpose, the loss - in nation after nation - of any sense of common solidarity that binds people across difference, the loss of those common stories and causes that foster community, mutuality, comradeship, and purpose."

It gets worse. Hyperindividualism "leads to a degradation and a pulverization of the human person," exploiting egoistic drives, encouraging over-the-top self-interest. The drives to seek connection through service to others is muted; the "longings of the heart and soul" are pushed aside in favor of "the desires of the ego." In the long run, he says, "Hyperindividualism creates isolated, self-interested monads who sense that something is missing in their lives but cannot even name what it is."

Consumerism plays no small role in this subversion, placing emphasis on material acquisition; meritocracy redefines "success" for the worse. Worst of all, hyperindividualism is "a network of conditional love," leading its practitioners to believe that love is earned, that worthiness to be loved is barter, and making them deeply sensitive to the judgments of others.

"When you build a whole society on an overly thin view of human nature," Brooks asserts, "you wind up with a dehumanized culture in which people are starved of the things they yearn for most deeply."

And it's making us all more tribal, he concludes: When the inherent meaninglessness of hyperindividualism triggers subconscious red alerts, the individual goes partisan, finding security in an Us and purpose in the channeling of their accumulated toxins of dissatisfaction and emptiness in the direction of a targeted Them.

All of this is pretty grim. But there is an alternative, Brooks suggests - a refocusing on those features of humanity that cannot be secured through hyperindividualism, but from a different way of thinking, a new approach to living that he called relationalism, which we will take up shortly.

None of the Above

A great many of our social issues and political conundrums are, upon examination, very complex. This makes for difficult discussion, let alone solution; human minds tend to embrace simplicity, rather than complexity, because our cognitive processing power is limited; the brain simplifies the world as it models it, as a coping mechanism – we come by it naturally.

But we have one another, and so we can, as a group, tackle the complexity that is so daunting to us as individuals.

A number of such issues loom before us. The 2019 arrest of Wikileaker Julian Assange is one.

The simplistic views of Assange's actions, which included felonious hacking and the release of a great deal of classified information – among other things - are many. Here are the most prominent ones.

Julian Assange is a hero: he has leaked information that exposed US military malfeasance, and in so doing, struck a blow for information transparency. No, that's too simple, because in doing so, he broke the law. Is that okay?

Julian Assange is a criminal: he leaked classified information and in so doing, committed felonies. No, that's too simple, because Assange (and fellow leaker Edward Snowden) made public information that exposed government actions that should not have remained hidden from public view.

More abstractly...

Whistleblowers who expose government malfeasance should celebrated, not punished: no, that's too simple; if individuals may arbitrarily decide what the public should and shouldn't know, then the reasons for classifying information - protection of individuals under threat; the rights of privacy of any number of persons involved; information that could empower a foreign enemy while weakening the US - go out the window, and US intelligence becomes a free-for-all.

Whistleblowers who expose government malfeasance should be punished, not celebrated: no, that's too simple; government actors often behave improperly, and those improprieties themselves can be dangerous and compromising, and often cost lives (see Ellsberg, Pentagon Papers) - it is right that such behavior be exposed, even if the disclosure violates the law.

Complicating the case of Julian Assange is the fact that he is an alleged conspirator, committing acts of espionage, and other felonies that call into question the purity of his motives.

Another complex issue is the Joe Biden "touching" issue, which occurred early in the 2019 presidential campaign.

The simplistic views of Biden's actions and the events we've subsequently seen are, likewise, many:

Joe Biden touched Nevada assemblyperson Lucy Flores inappropriately and without her permission, and this is unacceptable, and he should apologize: no, it's not that simple; it is easily demonstrated (and has been) that the specific incident that started the controversy 1) was in no way sexual, 2) was not specific to women (Biden routinely places his hands on the shoulders of men, as well), 3) had occurred in the past between Biden and Flores - the other way around (she placed her hand on *his* shoulder from behind without asking first). The claim, therefore, is disingenuous.

Joe Biden touched a woman he knew in a casual and inoffensive way, and her objection is purely political, to smear him unjustly, so he should not apologize: no, it isn't that simple; even if Flores is causing a political controversy for its own sake, and her claim is disingenuous, it is an unacceptable slippery slope to say that any individual may touch any other individual in any way without permission - while most contacts may be innocuous and inoffensive, we dare not open the door to those that are not.

In the abstract...

Some people are naturally affectionate, and the weaponizing of that affectionate expression for political purposes or otherwise degrades our society: no, it isn't that simple, for the reasons articulated above; yes, some people are naturally affectionate, while others are not - some people are huggers, and they come by those impulses naturally, and the impulses themselves are healthy ones; but some people are not, and their right to be left alone lives right alongside the rights of the huggers.

Some people are naturally intrusive, and their physical expressiveness should be discouraged, or all kinds of impropriety will break out: no, it isn't that simple; human beings are naturally physically connected, it is built into our genes, and is even the root source of our empathy (it originated in the skin-to-skin contact of anthropoid mother to anthropoid offspring in the act of breast-feeding, and persists in our bodies' exploitation of oxytocin - without it, we could not build the societies that sustain us).

I don't believe for a minute that Joe Biden is anything other than a good man whose natural affection and comfort with hugging and touch are a reflection of that goodness (my father is such a man, warm and kind and given to handshakes and hugs and reassuring pat on the back or arm-squeeze; I am not as at-ease as he is, but I wish I was). I also believe that the right of *any* individual, male or female, to be touched or not touched is sacrosanct. And I believe that societies that are more intimate, more open to human touch, and less easily offended and litigious are far healthier than our own.

I don't think this controversy is really about Joe Biden, in other words. But that's just me.

And my point is this: we can't simply choose One of the Above to satisfy our emotional cravings where complicated issues are concerned; if we are intellectually honest, we must choose None of the Above, and do the heavy lifting of crafting a new (and more complex) answer. To do less is unworthy of us.

The Original Humanists

Futurist Yuval Noah Harari has noted that the modern era, which has steadily increased the existential and spiritual self-sufficiency of humankind as religion has receded, faces the problem of infusing life with meaning in a post-religion world.

That challenge has been met, he writes, by humanism, which he defines as "a revolutionary new creed that conquered the world during the last few centuries...the humanist religion worships humanity, and expects humanity to play the part that God played in Christianity and Islam, and that the laws of nature played in Buddhism and Daoism."

"Whereas traditionally the great cosmic plan [of religion] gave meaning to the life of humans," he continues, "humanism reverses the roles and expects the experiences of humans to give meaning to the cosmos."

Humanism, he writes, creates meaning for a meaningless world; it calls upon us to draw the meaning of our own lives from our inner experiences, and then to extend that meaning to the universe as a whole. Humankind, in Harari's summary, is the author of meaning.

In his book *Homo Deus*, this idea is presented as the best path forward for humanity. But in reality, it is more; it's a return to the path we originally walked.

Religion has been with us for a little over 12,000 years, in the best guesses of modern anthropologists and evolutionary psychologists like Azim Shariff, who suggests that 'God' was invented when agriculture began at the end of the last Ice Age, and large communities became possible – communities where it was impossible to police the behaviors of all, making it necessary to invent an all-seeing, all-punishing policeman.

But humankind has been around far longer than 12,000 years. In our present form – homo sapiens – we've walked the earth for almost 300,000 years, and in less advanced form, ten times that long.

Were those thousands of centuries meaningless?

The millions of humans who lived and died in those years had brains like ours, communicated by language as we do (at least for the past 100,000 years or so), and built lives of shared experience, just like us. To read Harari without keeping this in mind is to passively assume that those millions of lives had no meaning – that "meaning", in the sense that we use it today, only came about with the invention of religion.

But is that even plausible?

The creation of meaning is built into the human brain. It isn't an invention of philosophers or poets or pastors; it's a natural function of the conscious mind. We are, each of us, makers of meaning.

This is why the question of meaning in our lives and in the universe around us matters so much in the first place: meaning necessarily exists in the mind, as it is an idea; and we all hunger for it, which tells us it's both natural and a function of mind.

If we've had it all along, then what *is* meaning, and where did it go?

The first clue can be found in the assumption that God(s) was/were ever a source of meaning; if we created God, then by definition, we are not only seekers of meaning – we are the *creators* of meaning. Our need for it follows our production of it.

Then we must accept that of all the life on Earth – as far as we know – and, for that matter, in all of time and space – as far as we are able to know – we are the only beings like ourselves to ever emerge, to ever get this far. We are on the leading edge of meaning; we are, in the universe, its sole source, its only repository.

Finally, we consider that while we may search for meaning as individuals, while we may each come up with solitary solutions in that quest, meaning itself is a community trait; when we find it, we share it, and it becomes a tying bind. Whatever distortions religion introduced into the nature and application of meaning, it positively underscores that meaning, by definition, is a group force. We create it together; we perceive it together; we enjoy it together. It nurtures us as one.

In our final analysis - *we* are meaning. We, humanity, *are meaning*. We *define* meaning. And if we've lost our innate sense of that, it's because our attention has been long diverted, obfuscated by emotional plunder and garish charlatanry.

We are not, then, robbing the gods. We are not overweening usurpers or pretenders in taking up Harari's call; we have always been his cosmic adjudicators, the chancellors of ultimate truth. Why? Because no others in creation can take up the task. It has always been ours. And we are, in the end, our own answer: humanity isn't taking meaning over; we're taking meaning back.

We are, after 10,000 years in the wilderness, returning to ourselves.

Clustered Hemispheres

We have often spoken of cognitive clustering – the gathering of like minds into closed circles of thought, where all assumptions are held in common, ideas need not be defended, and reason atrophies.

We have spoken of those clusters as being personality-driven, circles of attraction with handfuls of subconscious emotional tendencies at their center. No matter what their content, they are unhealthy and ultimately bring about their own decay.

When we read a few pages of British psychiatrist Iain McGilchrist, we quickly come up with a new take.

McGilchrist's concern is the differences between the hemispheres of the human brain. His study of those differences puts the lie to the decades-old clichés that have pervaded pop science – that "the left side is for reasoning, the right side is for feeling!", and so on. This is nonsense, McGilchrist has asserted: the two sides of the human brain do much the same things; they just do them differently.

The primary reason the brain in humans (and, in fact, in most animals) is divided into two halves is so that it can do two things at once: 1) pay attention to a survival task at hand (like catching food), while 2) paying attention to the surrounding environment (to avoid becoming something else's food).

Put another way, the left hemisphere is about attending to local details, while the right hemisphere is about maintaining the big picture.

McGilchrist put these thoughts together after studying, in excruciating detail, the behaviors of individuals who have suffered neurological damage – losing function in one hemisphere or the other. Invariably, such patients display a behavioral shift that reflects a cognitive dominance of the remaining hemisphere. That is, a person with right-brain damage will become detail-oriented, but lose the big picture; a person with left-brain damage will have a strong grasp of that big picture, but have little idea about how to accomplish tasks.

He also went out of his way, in his book *The Master and His Emissary*, to note how entire cultures are swayed in one direction or another when, at a macro scale, these two perspectives are out of balance. When a society biases too far away from big-picture thinking, and too deeply into the worship of details, it drifts into dysfunctionality. This, he says, is the pressing dilemma of the modern Western world.

This happens in nations because cognitive clusters are happening. Large associations of persons with left-brain bias are gathering into social groups; and right-brained persons are, as well. And so we have political groups that can't think more than a few months ahead on the one hand, and others that see the future clearly but can't solve social issues in the present. We've spawned religions that are bursting with simple answers to complex questions that don't apply to anything real, and philosophies that explain real things well but are devoid of forward motion.

We are, to put it simply, brain-damaged and paralyzed.

It is natural and even essential that we are not all in perfect balance, hemisphere-wise. Of course some of us will lean to the left brain, others to the right. That's a good and healthy thing. But it only serves us as a species when we all remain in balance socially, giving both left- and right-brained individuals their place in our social and cultural environment, as well as our political and policy processes.

We're already on the lookout for cognitive clusters, with the task of re-integrating with those who think differently. Now we add hemispheres to the list; when a group is too left- or too right-, nothing good ensues – it's time to mix it up.

ROI

Attention is not something we 'pay', it's something we invest. And the ROI is astounding.

The Cost of Knowledge

Anyone who has jumped through the burning hoops of graduate school knows the drill: knowledge begets knowledge, and when the knowledge is to emerge in a thesis or dissertation, the begetting knowledge must be painstakingly unearthed, like fossils in the Afar Triangle, from the endless strata of journals in a university library somewhere. Or from grueling, repetitive labwork. Or from even more grueling, often dangerous fieldwork.

Or, in lesser academic pursuits, from the World Book Encyclopedia, or anyone of five million other carefully vetted books.

Or, if one is a journalist, from prior publications, well-planned interviews, articulately documented events witnessed firsthand, or mountains of public records.

Or so it used to be.

This was, over the past two centuries, the cost of knowledge - the necessary investment required to extract reliable truth from the human record, in pursuit of its expansion. Since the earliest days of newspapers, public libraries and scientific publications, the acquisition of trustworthy knowledge has carried an often-significant personal energy cost.

That cost has been, historically, considerable. To learn, we require books or journals or something like them, written records of events and information and analysis and commentary to inform the learner - and that meant seeking those sources out, always at some personal expenditure of time and effort (in the case of academic pursuits, often Herculean effort).

This tremendous energy cost was exercise to the mind and character, strengthening the learner in myriad ways. And because of the cost of acquisition, the knowledge gained was held as precious, appreciated deeply as the product of personal industry and noble motivation. It had great value, not just for itself, but for the accomplishment of its attainment.

But no more. Those days are, to an unfortunate degree, over: this generation has experienced a breathtaking orders-of-magnitude drop in the cost of knowledge.

Today, as predicted by Arthur C. Clarke, all the world's computers are connected to one another in a gargantuan supernetwork of networks; today, as predicted by Isaac Asimov, all of that information is freely available in every home, to every woman, man, and child.

Any eight-year-old with an iPhone can acquire all the knowledge accessible to the most tenured professor, excepting academic papers stored behind paywalls (for that, the eight-year-old might have to pony up 25 bucks). Anyone who wishes to learn anything at all - from the rituals of the Druids to the details of brain surgery to the blueprints of the Gaza Pyramids - can do so at home on their couch in their underwear, whenever they choose. Anyone wishing to learn a new subject or skill - from quantum physics to behavioral genetics to Medieval literature - need only go to the public library, walk past all the books, and sit down at a freely-available, Internet-connected computer. All they must invest is the time it takes to read.

It is literally possible to amass the equivalent of a master's degree at no cost other than the investment of reading time: the cost of gaining access to the knowledge is literally now zero, in 99 percent of the cases we might posit.

This is a good thing, right?

By and large, yes. But it is fair to ask: what happens to the value of acquired knowledge, when the cost of acquiring it is so inconsequential?

Per the math we've hinted at above, that knowledge is no longer as precious to us. If we don't have to take any real effort to track down knowledge, we don't value it nearly as deeply.

Michael Crichton warns of this in his novel *Jurassic Park*. In the book, mathematician Ian Malcolm argues against the resuscitation of dinosaurs, stating that the genetic engineers of the park invested no effort in cultivating the knowledge to undertake the task - they simply exploited the work of others who had come before. They possess a frighteningly powerful technology, one that can revive the mightiest and most dangerous creatures that ever lived, but it required no discipline or sacrifice of them to obtain that power - only money.

We trust the martial artist who has the power to kill with his bare hands, Malcolm points out, because we realize he invested many years in developing his skill, resulting in the discipline and restraint to use it wisely. Is it not the same with knowledge?

We can ask, then, if the drive-thru knowledge now available via the Internet compromises us. And the answer must be, very probably. When we invest great effort in acquiring knowledge, we respect that knowledge; it takes a great deal to displace it, we don't give it up easily. When we invest only a few minutes in acquiring knowledge, it takes far less effort to dislodge it, to give competing information equal weight, because it is of equal personal cost.

When we must go to great effort to seek out information that is obscure, and then take pains to verify or validate it, we are strengthened by the undertaking; we develop a peripheral set of intellectual skills (and emotional responses) that fortify us, and our minds are improved. We must often be creative in our quest, when sources are few and hard to find. When it is at our fingertips, those skills go undeveloped.

It's hard to know what happens next. This is surely a two-edged sword, as the easy access of all the world's knowledge is inarguably a giant leap forward for humankind. But we're leaving something behind, and if we can't infuse knowledge with respect and value by way of the personal cost of attaining it, we must find another way.

For all the world's knowledge, at our fingertips, does us no good in the end if that respect and value fade away.

The Factual, Objective Answer

We stop searching for the factual, objective answer when we come across an answer that pleases us emotionally. Even scientists fall prey to this tendency (though they are caught and penalized when they do).

The Kavanaugh hearing in the fall of 2018 brought this out in high relief: we are seeing US senators demonstrating this truth – along with the media, the pundits, the party hacks, the guilty, the accusers, the spectators, the victims.

We become mature, fully self-actualized, productive human beings (and worthy citizens) when we learn to recognize this impulse and rise above it...

...when we insist to ourselves, I want to know the truth more than I want to be right...

... I want to know the truth, more than I want to feel good about the situation...

... I want to know the truth --- no matter what anyone else wants, or says, or thinks...

2069

Authoritarianism's Last Gasp, which characterizes our current moment, is exactly that. Coming to the brink of war, and by extension, extinction, brings about the strongest sense of international community ever achieved - and the drivers of climate upheaval and economic uncertainty turn even the oligarchs to the task of leveraging capitalism toward building new systems to prevent collapse, which in turn strengthen the weaker nations and solidify trade.

The instant gratification of the Internet spreads messages of prosperity in real time, putting the lie to the low-empathy folk ideologies that have been the rule through most of history: it becomes clear that where wealth is fairly distributed, economies flourish; where equality is defended, crime and exploitation whither; where human health and well-being are the leading state priorities, conflict is rare.

Human labor becomes less and less necessary as a component of these emerging social systems, as robotics and AI proliferate; public systems outpace private ones in accommodating human activity. AI, already the custodian of most business decisions, becomes humanity's servant in public policy and services.

Healthcare and education are free, the world over - human well-being has become the centerpiece of our social agenda. The idea that some people are better or more worthy or more deserving than others has begun to fade from the human story, as three generations of children have grown up watching Others in real time, and know from the age they can walk and speak that the concept of privilege is bullshit.

Big Tobacco, Big Pharma and the Big Banks are all gone, as AI has outperformed all the private drug companies combined, in coming up with new medicine, delivered economic models that out-perform the finance industry by an order of magnitude, and have generated cures for every human addiction.

We are terraforming Mars and have cities on the moon, where the low gravity is extending the lives of tens of thousands who would be dead otherwise.

Capitalism is not dead; it is alive and thriving, as the human social system lavishly rewards innovation. But it has been removed from all equations where human well-being is at stake. Religion is likewise alive and well, protected by law – provided it does not indulge in social dominance.

Authority is democratically assumed, all across the world - and elections are sacrosanct. Severe prison terms await those who would usurp another's vote, by any means, or intimidate another person in their pursuit of their civic participation. AI is watchdog here, as well, and has made the systems that manage the election of government representatives secure. Socially, harm to another's ability to participate in government is considered more egregious than physical attack.

Similarly, harm to ecosystems is considered a crime against humanity, and laws protecting them are harsh. Yet again, AI is watchdog, not only overseeing the security of natural air and water systems and sanctuaries, but modeling for their optimization. Poverty is long gone; crime and corruption are still possible, but very difficult; populations have balanced out, as control has been incentivized and health education has become ubiquitous. Cancer is gone, as are most diseases.

Finally, patriarchy is dead. Men and women oversee humankind together, as partners. Family life has expanded to take many new shapes and forms. Women have full control of their own destinies - and men and women alike have social roles available to them that suit their natural cognitive inclinations. Put another way, there are paths to happiness available to all.

That's my vision.

What's yours?

In God We Trust

For most of the time human beings have existed, we did just fine without religion. It's a pretty recent invention, as cultural innovations go, and the need for it simply didn't exist before.

Why not?

Until about 12,000 years ago, human being existed in very small communities – traveling groups of a hundred people or so. Everyone knew everyone else, from birth till death (which came all too quickly in predator-filled Africa); everyone was kin, to some degree, and each member of the tribe was family-familiar. We lived and died together, in those days.

Consequently, it would have been next to impossible to get away with bad behavior: in such small groups, it was not difficult to hold everyone to account. And there was great incentive to offer the group our very best efforts.

Put another way, Nature imbued early human society (2,500 centuries of it) with community that equaled, and probably far surpassed, the fellowship and moral behaviors we loosely associate with religious communities today.

What changed? Why did we go from implicitly spiritual communities to explicitly religious ones?

It turns out, per Canadian psychologist Azim Shariff, that religion emerged as a "cultural innovation" that was an effective fix to a sudden and serious problem.

When the earth warmed at the end of the last Ice Age cycle, and new mutant grasses brought about the beginnings of agriculture, human communities ceased to be nomadic and began to settle in fixed locations. Until that time, the traveling groups of 100 or so had been in perfect social balance, because the number of people in a human tribe was more or less the number of relationships the human cortex can intellectually and emotionally process effectively. (This number is called Dunbar's Number, and applies to all higher primate species.)

But with fixed communities, that number began to grow much higher - to 200, 500, even 1,000 members, several thousands of years before the first modest city-states emerged. With populations like those, it was no longer possible to know every individual in the community like family. It was possible to walk alongside a complete stranger - something that had never before occurred.

Before fixed human communities, trust between community members was a given; when fixed communities appeared, trust became much, much shakier.

Individuals could now cheat the group, in terms of taking more than their share, or shirking responsibility, or failing to abide by the standards that kept communities safe from predators. There were no all-seeing individuals to catch acts of malfeasance, and no means of punishing perpetrators.

And into this vacuum, Shariff suggests, stepped religion.

Problems with cheaters? Apparent, and growing. Able to observe and intervene? Not nearly enough. Punish them? Some, but not nearly all.

The "cultural innovation", Shariff asserts, is the creation of an all-knowing punisher or two. Or three. Or more, depending on the community. An omniscient, omnipotent enforcer to stem the tide of theft and malfeasance: God(s).

Not surprisingly, this turned out to be exceedingly effective, at least where the original intent goes: having a religion in place enforces conformity to social behavioral standards in the society that adheres to it. 'Trust' becomes a matter of religious identity; if an individual unknown to me approaches, but demonstrates membership in the religion I embrace, I confer trust upon that individual by default.

It goes without saying that this 'trust' is as flimsy as swimwear in the Bahamas, but it works at least somewhat reliably for the purposes intended. When communities began to trade with other communities, the emergence of commerce was softened by religious markers. Expectations of fairness and honesty, based on religious identity displays, increased the efficacy of trade and the spread of the religion. It became easier to deal with strangers and expect an equitable outcome.

The serpent in the garden, Shariff goes on to point out, is that this dynamic can backfire: if we are conditioned to inherently trust an individual we don't know who is of our religion, we are conversely conditioned to suspect (and even reject) an individual who is not, despite their actual level of trustworthiness. In other words, religious markers as a 'trust' cue have replaced actual trust cues. And, of course, we trip right over that phenomenon every single morning of every single day, the instant we glance at our news feeds.

Now distrust has surpassed trust in the equation of human interaction. Now we have wars. Dominance. Inequality. Bigotry.

Is all of this a consequence of religion? No, of course not; it is not the fault of religion that human communities grew beyond the capacity of our minds to manage them; it is not the fault of religion that its practitioners seldom have the knowledge or experience to distinguish between conferred trust and actual trust. But the religions of the world, both ancient and modern - or more specifically, their leaders - have much to answer for, having learned the trust equation and exploited it, not for the good of the community but for darker agendas. It's one thing to misappropriate trust; it's another to cultivate distrust. The former absconds with the fruits of the human collective; the other destroys it altogether.

And where is 'God' in all of this? Where He's always been: in the voice and schemes and desires of his spokesmen, imposing His will - diminishing and weakening those He was invented to save, eroding the goodness and potential of the souls that gave Him birth.

It's Personal

Cognitive clustering - the self-selection of a group into a collective of like-mindedness - can be characterized as perhaps the single greatest destructive force to civilized humanity since... well, civilization. It is the root cause of war, the most despicable religions, fascism and totalitarianism, patriarchy (and thereby misogyny), bigotry. Whatever human social toxin you might call out, it takes but a glance to spot a cognitive cluster at its heart.

It's a huge problem, and fixing it on a macro scale is a daunting undertaking. There is no solution that does not itself seem totalitarian.

But if we can't easily change human groups, we remain deeply empowered to change cognitive clustering within ourselves, as individuals - by de-clustering.

How can a personal cognitive de-clustering occur? Through the systematic, committed pursuit of cognitive diversity. Here are some thoughts.

Invite others in. Odds are you belong to several cognitive clusters - a church, a political party, a circle of friends who reflect your own social and political ideas. People who already live within your comfort zone.

Expand those groups. Invite someone you know into the group, knowing ahead of time that they won't be a perfect fit, that they won't share the collective view and opinions of the group. Make it your mission to create a safe space for the newcomer, to be an active agent of inclusion and connection, stepping in when others might push in a negative way against the new person's differing perspective. This effort will accomplish a great deal: it will boost personal awareness within the group; it will be good social and emotional exercise for you, working to be a bridge-builder; it will be a positive undertaking for the other group members, practicing inclusion; and it will make the newcomer feel valued.

Join an Out-group. Undertake the same experience from the other side. Seek out, through a friend, a social group you wouldn't otherwise think to join, and that wouldn't think to include you. Do so with the intent of exploring and understanding that group and its members, realizing that they will test your own worldview. Do so in pursuit of human connection, beyond those differences that have traditionally been barriers.

Conspire with the friend you approach for the introduction, explaining what you're doing; let that person, who already knows you, serve as a bridge. And when you arrive in this new group, put aside any thoughts of pushing your own ideas or tearing down anyone else's; make your mission one of belonging, not persuading.

This effort will also have numerous benefits: it will help you clarify those things that you believe, and give you a deeper understanding of why others don't always share your beliefs. It will put the lie to many distortions that your usual in-groups have layered across others, strengthening your filters for those times when you're back in your tribe; and it will boost your sense that there is more than unites us than divides us.

Read an Other book. Exploring cognitive diversity isn't always a matter of group activity. Sometimes it's simply watching and listening in places you normally don't.

Read a book by a commentator who caters to people who don't think like you. If you think Libertarians are kooks, read Jordan Peterson's book. If you think liberal atheists are out to destroy all that's holy, read Sam Harris; if you've never been able to stomach the Right, check out George Will.

Explain yourself. One of the ways that cognitive clusters damage us, even when their collective views are socially benign, is by removing our need to articulate our reasoning and emotions. We simply state our position and it's accepted, because the others in the group already share it. That leads to a destructive atrophy of our ability to process - and, just as importantly - the why of our perspective.

Make it a practice to restore this aspect of self-expression. Even when you're among those of like mind, add a comment that supports your opinion, beyond its expression. And lean toward support that would make sense to someone not of your in-group. This is not only healthy mental exercise for you, and a strengthening of your own reasoning - it encourages the same in others. Odds are that if you express a view you know will be shared by your group, but add some support to it, someone else will chime in with a similar supporting comment, and you might learn something new. Or, alternately, they might question your supporting comment, which will (productively) prompt you to re-think it.

Challenge your ding. All human beings of all tribes, regardless of stripe or domain, have a switch built into their brains: the dopamine ding. It's a 'rightness' alert that goes off when the brain is satisfied with the inputs it's receiving.

The dopamine *ding* isn't just about reasoning and opinion; it goes off when we have a drink, a hit of weed, a great roll in the hay. It signals all is well.

The problem is, the *ding* originated tens of millions of years back in evolution, long before we even developed cortical tissues (for reasoning and social processing). Ancient *ding* triggers tend to override more modern, sophisticated ones: for instance, a jacked-up imaginary threat (*Aliens are among us! Christians will hang all gays! Liberals are coming for your guns!*) that requires an understanding of modern social dynamics to even parse will set off a fear response not unlike being told there's a Bengal tiger loose in your neighborhood.

Preachers, politicians and pundits all know this, and so flip the *ding* switch of unsuspecting listeners constantly, as a means of manipulating them.

The very nature of the *ding* inclines us to trust it - even when we definitely shouldn't. It can become a healthy practice, then, when we feel that little twinge of satisfaction at hearing an idea we agree with or making a decision that 'feels right', to pause and do a reality check. It costs us nothing to double-check the *ding,* and when we make this a habit, the *ding* itself will go off less often and more reliably.

Try ideas out. When we puzzle over a decision, or find the world ambiguous and are sorting through what our feelings are telling us about a troubling event, we tend to turn to those who have reinforced our ideas in the past. And that, of course, sets up a feedback loop of bias.

By all means, run an idea past an in-group friend. And you'll undoubtedly get a dopamine *ding* when you do, as you have in the past (it's what urges you to return to that friend for opinions). But, as suggested above, don't buy into that ding; instead, push through it and proceed to one or two others beyond your group, friends who won't rubber-stamp your reasoning or your feelings. Accept the additional input, compare opinions side-by-side, process everything - and then move toward a position. You may end up where you were to begin with, but you'll have become a little stronger along the way.

Vary your pattern. Finally - mix it up.

The human brain goes for simplicity, just because the world is so relentless in thrusting new information into it. We embrace the comfort of sameness, the ease of routine.

But pushing against sameness and routine, even when our brains are naturally predisposed toward it (and some brains are, more so than others), makes our minds stronger. If we develop the habit of changing our habits, we cultivate a brain that can more easily grow and change and adapt. It also imparts more control of how and when those changes and adaptations occur.

This breaking of routine need not be in the realm of ideas and emotions: it's all neurons and synapses up there, and any focused effort to boost situational awareness boosts the mind's decision-making focus. So eat something different for breakfast; choose a new route to the office; shave left-to-right instead of right-to-left. Mix it up.

Diet of the Mind

We are a diet-obsessed bunch, aren't we? The more we learn about carbs and cholesterol and cardio and cortisol, the more frightening fast food feels. (See what I did there?)

And while we're obsessing, paying too much for specially-labeled groceries and gym memberships, counting our steps and tracking BMI and cramming meals into feeding windows, we're neglecting our most nutrition-conscious organ: our brains!

The brain operates by the same general principles as the body: healthy input equals healthy outcomes! Eat right, feel great! And, of course, on the flip side - garbage in, garbage out: cheeseburgers and chili dogs will not a long life make.

Put good, healthy stuff in the mind, and the mind will perform very well, generating strong thoughts, good decisions, a fruitful worldview and a balanced perspective. Nibble at the stupid, however, and stupid the mind becomes.

Even the folks who give the most rigorous attention to what they put into their bodies seldom give any serious thought to what they're putting into their brains. As a result, we are a nation of fat, weak, lazy thinkers, barely able to generate enough energy to get off the cognitive couch, let alone out into the intellectual sunlight for a jog.

Fortunately, your Uncle Scott is on the job! Here's a quick dietary guide for hungry minds, to steer you around the crap and into some real nutrition!

The Sugar of the Mind

Confirmation bias is to the mind as sugar is to the sweet tooth: an endless craving for the yummy sweetness of our own opinions! The body hankers for sweet things because sugars represent quick energy, a survival advantage in our challenging past. So strong is our longing for sweets that we often can't say No, even when we know we should.

Similarly, our minds crave rightness, because being right was once the difference between living and dying – so any tickle of the brain that makes us feel we're right is as yummy as sugar. We can't say No, even when we ought to.

The Pork Rinds of the Mind

Cognitive dissonance to the mind as pork rinds are to the palate; appearing as bacon to the eye, registering as salted outdoor grill scrapings to the tongue, they are a sensory train wreck – they knock the mind full tilt, as one set of readings battles the other for the snacker's attention.

The Big Gulps and Popcorn Tubs of the Mind

Who among us hasn't tossed their diet aside when going to the movies with friends? We love sinking back into those comfy seats with our big, sugary soft drinks, passing around a big tub of buttery popcorn.

Our minds work the same way! When we get together with friends for some common purpose, all synced up, all on the same page, all cognitively clustered, we pass around some bucket of buttery ideas that everybody loves, gorging ourselves on tasty consensus.

Where do we go for such gooey, messy treats? Political parties spring to mind...

The Fast Food of the Mind

The body loves a routine that includes the fully-satisfying quick hit – a burger and fries, maybe chicken tenders and onion rings, something that feels kind of like a meal and relieves those hunger pangs without all the fuss of, you know, nutrition! We become addicted to this easy satisfaction, making it an all-too-frequent ritual for its convenience and broad accessibility.

Religion is the fast food of the mind. It serves up answers to all our worries, from the niggling to the ponderous, neatly bundled in combos on easy-order menus! It's instant gratification on steroids, sparing us the trouble of preparing or processing any substance or meaning, to say nothing of not having to go out and gather the ingredients of answers on our own.

The Chocolate of the Mind

Some things, diet-wise, are healthy in small doses. Indulge a bit in the proper context, and you've done your body right; indulge a lot, without context, and you've done your body harm.

Chocolate stands out as the most popular exemplar: it is super-yummy, appealing in taste, scent and texture, and comes in many varieties. It goes well with so many other delights, it's hard to list them all. Yet too much chocolate corrupts the metabolism, interrupting the body's healthy functioning and overturning the consumer's nutritional balance; it becomes a gateway to other damaging indulges.

So it is with philosophy: in modest doses, it stimulates and energizes, and can be enjoyed alongside a host of other healthy mental satiations. But too much, unaccompanied, is an invitation to intellectual paunch and sloth.

The Red Wine of the Mind

We can sing endlessly of the virtues of red wine: it invigorates every meal, warms every occasion; per Byron, it "cheers the sad, revives the old, inspires the young, makes weariness forget his toil"; it is "the most civilized thing in the world." It is grand, it is classic, it is timeless.

Poetry aside, it does do a couple of nice things; it calms the mind and is somewhat heart-healthy, and there is mild evidence that it slows aging.

And then it turns into sugar, screwing up the metabolism, taking over all thought and distorting perception and perspective all to hell.
Mythology is the red wine of the mine. It is grand, classic, timeless; invigorating and inspiring, and appropriate across a broad range of discourse. But living in it blurs the vision and balance of the

intellect, makes you dizzy as hell, and causes you to forget more important things.

The Keto Diet of the Mind

The trendy, healthy balance of the body at this particular culture moment is the Keto Diet, which manages blood sugar by limiting the consumption of carbohydrates, much as the Atkins Diet did a generation ago. It overturns low-fat, calorie-counting thinking by focusing on metabolism, raising the awareness of its practitioners in the domain of macronutrients.

It resembles the Paleo Diet, in that it puts protein out front (as our ancient ancestors did), minimizing sugars and starches (which weren't abundant in the environment 100,000 years ago).

Yet it is dangerous to do all the time: too much protein can cholesterol levels and cause serious kidney problems. The body needs at least some carbohydrates to balance out the protein.

It's the same with the mind. The ingestion of protein, nutritionally, is the exploitation of energy consumed by other creatures; our minds can do the same, absorbing the knowledge of those who came before. A high-protein diet of the mind, then, is the steady intake of knowledge.

We have a place for that meal, even in the Internet age: the public library!

But, as with the Keto Diet, it can't be just protein, all the time: a healthy mind isn't just a mind full of knowledge - experience counts for much. That doesn't come from books.

The Keto Diet of the Mind, then, works like its namesake: it's something you should do regularly - as often as possible! - but you can't do it full time and live in the world.

Money, Guns, and Dildos

For all the gun lobby's endless ranting about the Second Amendment and the citizen's right to fight back against the Big Bad Gub'mint (the same gub'mint it paradoxically wants to give $75 billion more for weapons every year), we know that the $$$ is what it's really all about: curbing America's appetite for firearms would seriously diminish the bottom line of gun manufacturers.

And so it comes as no surprise to learn that in Arizona – where they do love their guns! - it is perfectly legal for the average citizen to buy as many guns as s/he pleases and keep them in the home.

It is *illegal* in Arizona, however, for the average home in Arizona to contain more than two dildos[2].

Let's think about this a bit. Per the NRA, and Arizona law, there is no harm to society if – and citizens' rights are preserved when – guns in the home are legally unconstrained; but it *is* harmful to society, and citizens have no right to, more than two dildos per household.

I think we can see what's going on here, can't we? There are two possibilities: either that third dildo represents a credible threat, against which there is no constitutional defense – or somebody's trying to regulate the dildo industry.

Can you imagine how dildo manufacturers must feel about this? I am certain they must be up in arms – so to speak! - but can only surmise that they have made no countermove because of the obvious rhetorical challenges.

My solution? Use the gun lobby's own words against them! Consider: we see noise about gun rights and gun laws and gun control and gun legislation all over the place, right? We can underscore the absurdity of dildo control by (wait for it) using the language of gun control!

---

[2] In Texas, it's six. They think big in Texas…

Consider – what would the headlines look like?

Dildo politics in the United States

**_Democrats to Use CDC Report to Argue
Dildos Are 'A Public Health Risk'_**

White House, Congress taking 'baby steps' on dildo control

Dildo rights vs. Dildo control

Headlines concerning public opinion:

How do Americans feel about dildo control?

**_Gallup polls conducted from 2007 to 2012 found the following
levels of self-declared dildo ownership among different groups
of people_**

Headlines concerning legislation:

House lawmakers prepare rollout of dildo control agenda

**_Dildo News of the Week: Dildo Control Restrictions Will Imperil
the Nation's Defense Industries_**

Trump administration bans bump stocks for dildos

Why states, not Congress, are passing more dildo laws

**_Nancy Pelosi: House will pass bipartisan dildo legislation
"soon" after new House is seated_**

House Democrats Gear Up to Introduce Their First Dildo Control Bill of the New Congress

Democrats plan to pursue most aggressive dildo control legislation in decades

Headlines concerning statistics:

Hand dildos comprised 52% of all new dildos sold to civilians and law enforcement in 2014, as compared to 35% in 2000

Civilians accounted for 80% of non-military dildo industry revenues in 2012

Headlines concerning activism:

What the Anti-Dildo Agenda Doesn't Want You to Know

Privacy groups oppose state dildo control proposal

International headlines:

How US dildo control compares to the rest of the world

How Brazil's New President Will Prove, Yet Again, That Dildo Control is Harmful

Dildo control is Nazi-occupied France

Headlines concerning societal impact:

The racist roots of dildo control

Black people are left out of the dildo control debate

See what I mean? The dildo lobby, it seems, has its work cut out for it...

Relationalism

Earlier, we looked at the Second Mountain concept put forth by conservative thinker David Brooks, who renounced right-wing tribalism in search of deeper truths about the state of Western society and how a healthier cultural balance might be achieved.

This concept includes his renouncing of *hyperindividualism* - the social impetus to indulge the self to the exclusion of more human pursuits, which Brooks argues has utterly permeated society and culture.

The remedy he puts forth - his Second Mountain – he calls *relationalism*. Here's what it means.

"We are formed by relationship, and we long for relationship," he explains. "Life is not a solitary journey. It is building a home together. It is a process of being formed by attachments and then forming attachments in turn. It is a great chain of generations passing down gifts to one another."

He compares and contrasts hyperindividualism and relationalism. The former is "a collection of individuals who contract with one another," while the latter is "a web of connections that in many way precedes choice."

Society needs a "moral ecology" that supersedes hyperindividualism, where "We" overrides "Me", a "creed that puts relation, not the individual, at the center, and which articulates, in clear form, the truths we all know."

Among these truths: "Life is a qualitative endeavor, not a quantitative one"; "The best adult life is lived by making commitments and staying faithful to those commitments"; "The beautiful life is found in the mutual giving of unconditional gifts".

He asserts that relationalism is the path between hyperindividualism, with its sterile detachment, and collectivism, with its crushing of the soul in a faceless herd. The middle ground, per Brooks, "is not a system of ideas," but a way of life, in which each person "seeks to build a neighborhood, nation, and world of diverse and creative people who have made commitments in a flowering of different ways, who are nonetheless bound together by sacred chords."

"The hyperindividualist operates by a straightforward logic: I make myself strong and I get what I want," he summarizes; "The relationalist says, Life operates by an inverse logic. I possess only when I give. I lose myself to find myself. When I surrender to something great, that's when I am strongest and most powerful."

Right is Left and Left is Right

British psychiatrist Iain McGilchrist has summarized for us the differences between the hemispheres of the brain, putting the lie to outdated popular notions of "Left=Reason, Right=Creativity" and so on. His work, which extends the solid research of many others and includes studies of his own patients, as well as numerous subjects who experienced damage to one hemisphere or the other, demonstrates that the two hemispheres of the human brain (all mammalian brains, really) don't exactly do different things – they do the same things differently.

Primarily, each hemisphere generates a version of reality. The job of the right hemisphere is to capture a 'big picture' portrait of that reality, while the job of the left is to create an in-the-moment snapshot, focused on an immediate task. The reason for this division of labor is simple: the survival of all creatures requires two simultaneous missions – 1) eat, and 2) don't get eaten. The left hemisphere handles the immediate, tactile job of obtaining and consuming food; the right monitors the environment for threat and opportunity, as well as adding Past and Future to the left's Present.

That's simple and clear, we can agree. But it's also enormously complex, once we dive in.

The resulting tendencies in cognition, emotion, and behavior become clear when one hemisphere takes the lead:

Left Brain

Intense focus, the purpose of which is success in gathering food quickly and efficiently;

Focus on the moment, the immediate task at hand;

Literalism - one term, one meaning, to avoid confusion and ambiguity;

Knowledge - information essential to task completion;

An algorithmic approach to values – consequences, not circumstances, because outcome is the immediate priority;

Anger is the primary emotion, as input from others is a distraction, not a help, and threatens task completion;

Awareness of itself: the left brain is unaware of the right brain, because awareness of the right brain would overburden and distract the left from its mission.

Right Brain

General awareness, because tracking events in the environment requires the broadest possible attention;

The past and future, because awareness of both informs the brain's search for threat and opportunity;

Metaphor - This is like *That* is the core of learning, to improve performance over time;

Understanding - The incorporation of knowledge into a broader framework, so that new information breeds increased competence;

A holistic approach to values – circumstances, not consequences, because performance improvement is the long-term priority;

Empathy is the primary emotion, because a global awareness of the environment includes sensitivity to the emotions and behaviors of others as learning opportunities;

Awareness of itself, awareness of left: the right brain is constantly aware of both its own operation and the activities of the left, because global awareness is its function.

(It's important to note, reviewing the lists above, that they are about functionality – and not just functionality, but *survival*. They are, each and all, essential to staying alive and thriving in a very dynamic world. As such, we can't look at any one of them and say it is good or bad – just essential.)

Put simply, if we generalize these cognitive and behavioral tendencies to contemporary human society, we see the Left

Brain features as those defining the extremes of the political Right, and the Right Brain features as the extremes of the political Left. Right is Left and Left is Right, when it comes to sociopolitical tendencies and division of brain function.

Left World, Right World

In a recent podcast interview, McGilchrist was asked what the world would be like if everyone on the planet was Left-Brained, or if everyone was Right-Brained.

Left:

"Well, obviously, we would lose sight of the big picture," he replied. "That's the thing I've emphasized throughout. There'd be an emphasis on the details, instead. There would be a great emphasis on predictability, organizability, anonymity, categorization, loss of the unique and an ability to break things down into parts but not really see what the whole is like. There'd be a need for total control because the left hemisphere is somewhat paranoid. After right hemisphere damage, people often develop a paranoia, and that's because one can't understand quite what's going on and one needs, therefore, to control it. Anger would become the key note in public discourse. Everything would become black and white.

"The left hemisphere needs to be decisive because, don't forget, it's the one that's catching the prey. It's no good at going, well, yeah, it could be a rabbit, but it might not be. It's going to go, I'm going to go for it. So it likes black and white. It doesn't like shades of meaning. So in this world, we would lose the capacity to see grades of difference. We would misunderstand everything that is implicit and metaphorical and have to make rules about how to achieve it."

And if the whole world went Right-Brained,

"The right hemisphere, if it were really without the left hemisphere, would see a lot of connections between things and would see a broad picture, but it might not be so good at focusing on details," he said. "Emotionally, the timbre might be somewhat melancholic and sad. Because I think it's one of the aspects, I'm afraid, of the right hemisphere's realism and sympathy, a capacity for empathy, that it does feel suffering. We would not be able to make calculations in the same way. Most arithmetic calculations are made by the left hemisphere.

"So we would be good at coming up with ideas. We might not be good at actually sort of carrying out the nuts and bolts and getting it working as a machine."

Is any of this seeming familiar?

Sure enough, McGilchrist commented on how the world we live in today is leaning increasingly toward Left-Brain thinking:

"I think what I observe is an overemphasis on predetermined systems of algorithms," he said, "The sense of social alienation. The way in which we live divorced from the natural world, which is a very new phenomenon. The insistence on extreme positions, which is what the left hemisphere understands, not a nuanced argument about the pros and cons of every single thing.

"Meaning comes out of living in a consistent culture where there is a sense of connection with one's past. And not just one's own past, but the past of the people who made you who you were, with the other people in the society to which you belong and to the world at large. The natural world and things that are just simply beyond our ken, the transcendental. These are very important things that the right hemisphere's much better equipped to understand, and I feel the loss of them in modern life is grievous."

Full circle

This new understanding of how the brains we are born with define the people we become, our thoughts, our viewpoint, our behavior and emotions, can generate tremendous insights into why the world has become as confusing and disheartening as it has in recent decades: as we increasingly huddle into clusters of like-mindedness, we set up high-gain loops of Left Hemisphere Thinking and Right Hemisphere Thinking – Right-wing extremism and Left-wing extremism.

And the lessons of McGilchrist's research should inform not only our insights but our compassion: did you *choose* your dominant hemisphere? Did you *choose* global over local, or literalism over metaphor, or any particular focus? Or is it just how your individual brain rolls, the play of the genes you were born with?

And even if you had chosen, even if you had woken up one day and said, "I'm gonna be a Lefty Brain!" or "I'm feelin' like a Righty!", isn't it agonizingly clear that whichever way you lean, we need both sides – *working together closely!* - to survive?

The long-term success of humankind requires that we get in touch with our own minds, understanding *why* we think and feel and act as we do – and, just as importantly if not more – why *others* think and feel and act as they do.

Put another way, understanding Left Brain/Right Brain can lower the judgmental attitudes we are currently indulging in, and restore some of the natural balance that nature has laid at our feet.

By the very science we have just reviewed, this step will be much harder for a left-brained person. But the response of the right-brained person should not be a withdrawal of their natural empathy, or (worse yet) to begin echoing the left brain's intense (and perfectly natural) self-indulgence: all this does is diminish the right-brained person's ability to maintain the big picture.

The best thing we can do, in restoring nature's balance, is to un-cluster ourselves, socially – if right-brained people spend more time with left-brained people, and vice versa, each begins to strengthen the other, and we all wind up stronger in the long run.

Otherwise, there won't be a long run.

Generation Z

I had a long talk with my daughter yesterday. For more than a decade, we have reserved early Saturday for lunch and a hike, and yesterday our conversation turned to our respective generations.

I noted that while every upcoming generation tends to shift left of the one in power, her generation (she's 18, Gen Z) is not simply questioning the institutions that mine (the Boomers) have perpetuated, they are already summarily rejecting many of them.

Young people in the US are calling BS all around us, but not in the idealistic fog of the 1960s hippies; they are far more cynical than we ourselves.

I asked her about this: what is Gen Z's take on human nature, and how does it factor into your own expectations about the future that's possible for you? Her answer surprised me.

She and her peers, she said, are the first generation to grow up completely in the Internet - that's true, of course - and as a consequence, they achieved a far more complete model of the world at a far earlier age than we did. From the time they could hold an iPad, they were deeply immersed in the ceaseless barrage of information about their culture, the society in which they were swimming, the world around it, and what everybody thinks about everything.

All of her young life, she has been inundated with the following:

-Unending tribal warfare: the Right hating the Left and the Left hating back; Gen Z was born well after the era of Gingrich Smackdown that ended bipartisan cooperation);

-Open and unrestrained win-at-all-costs: while my generation was taught that We, The People own our political process, at least in principle, hers has had a front-row seat to unabashed gerrymandering, voter suppression and shameless stacking of the deck;

-War on Others: the bigotry and misogyny that used to happen in shadows are now paraded in banner headlines;

-The end of civility: my daughter has never known a time when the default in public discourse was courtesy and deference – she was raised on toxic clickbait where systematic character assassination is the norm;

-Fox News.

For more than 25 years now, all of this has been served up to their young eyes and ears daily, with complete indifference to the effects it might have on their perception of their society, their nation, their place in the world and their sense of their own future.

This is our horrific legacy. It seems a little extreme when it's me and Josie, separated by not one but two generations (I was 40 when she was born), but these contrasts are very real and very troubling, regardless of where one sits in the timeline.

Generation Z has never seen a Tip O'Neill. Or a Dorothy Height. Or an Alice Walker. Or a Walter Cronkite. Decency and grace in public discourse had long since been abandoned before they ever learned to surf the net. Men and women who were pillars of integrity, champions of adulting, are no longer held up to our youth; they simply aren't interesting enough, in the Internet age, to draw clicks.

I wish I could say I absorbed her answer with thoughtful perception and was able to render an insightful, encouraging response. But the awkward truth is that I had nothing.

I don't know what to say to Generation Z. And any words I might muster would sound hollow, I'm sure. The young people around us are as smart as we ever were, and the ground around them is littered with evidence of our shallowness, our short-sightedness, our apparent abandonment of self-awareness. They don't think we have much to offer them; they don't think we've given them much consideration. They don't think much of what we've built. And they come by these opinions very honestly.

I look at my daughter as she opens the front door, preparing to step out of it, and I'm ashamed.

I have much work still to do, and almost no time left to do it.

Thermohaline

Regarding global warming, and climate change in general, I have been asked many times how it is that if the Earth is warming too quickly because of our damage to the atmosphere, how is it we are speeding up the next Ice Age cycle?

It works like this: a huge component of the warm spell we have enjoyed over the past 13,000 years, since the last retreat of glacial ice sheets, has been thermohaline circulation - the flow of the oceans (the Atlantic in particular), which carry warm salty water north and cool salty water south. This even distribution of heat has kept the climate of the planet mild overall, which is of course very good for our species - we have thrived, these past 13,000 years.

It works much like the flow of coolant in an engine, and is an example of what I've lately been calling the England Imperative, the impetus of natural systems to organize in such a way as to spread energy.

Now, then: what happens if the thermohaline circulation shuts down? What if that spreading of energy, that distribution of heat brought on by the ocean currents, ceases? We plunge back into cold; glaciers would re-emerge, the Earth would receive less sunlight (because more and more of it would be reflected back into space - ice-albedo feedback - as the glaciers grew), and we'd be back to hunting mammoth to survive (No, wait...).

The question becomes, how could thermohaline circulation be shut down? The melting of glacial ice is the primary cause, along with atmospheric shifts brought on by ozone depletion. How do we know? Because it's happened at least 21 times in the course of the last Ice Age, leaving its marks in ice and ground core samples all over the world.

What can we do?

Start listening to scientists, and stop listening to politicians. Stop thinking about today, and start thinking about tomorrow...

The Truth

For quite some time, a particular social group has kept itself in place as the ruling class in the Western world. In this age of instant communication, global economics and the heightened awareness that technology provides, this ruling class is finally falling – and it is fighting back against its fall with all its might.

But certain unassailable truths stand in the path of these struggling dominators – moral truths, to be sure, or truths that can be distorted through the use of certain rhetorical calisthenics – but more than that, scientific truths: empirical reality, unbendable by human will.

The Truth:

Human females are as intelligent, as competent and capable, as moral, as artistic, as mature, and as able to decide wisely and act effectively as human males. For all the efforts of human males to distort these truths about human females over the millennia, it is now unassailable.

The Truth:

The color of a human being's skin is of no consequence with respect to that person's intelligence, competence, character, emotional depth or potential; skin color is an evolutionary adaptation to the intensity of sunlight in various regions of the earth, nothing more. For all the efforts of humans of one color to disparage humans of another, this truth is unassailable.

The Truth:

Human beings are the Swiss Army Knife of life on Earth: we are each of us (and every one of us) capable of wonders, compared to our fellow creatures. The differences between human beings are infinitesimal compared to the vast gulf separating us from all the others.

Men and women are equal.

Persons of all colors are equal.

The rule of one gender over the other, the rule of one color over all the others, is at an end. It has brought us only strife and pain and diminished lives; it should never have happened in the first place.

Science and the Octants

Science is the ultimate Authoritarian: it stands firmly above all other ways of knowing, secure in its objectivity, its rigor, its unassailable integrity. It tolerates no fraud, it suffers no pretenders. It stands alone in its authority, eschewing any epistemological democracies - unapproached and unapproachable by lesser, more casual ventures.

Science is the ultimate Egalitarian: it is no respecter of persons, but gives equal time and opportunity to all. The highest human authority can whither under its scrutiny, while the lowliest inquirer can topple mountains. The evidence is all; the investigator, merely its courier.

Science scans relentlessly for Threat: it is poised for assault from all quarters, hunkered down in barracks fortified relentlessly over centuries, anticipating attack from anywhere at any time; it proceeds on the assumption that the viral weaknesses of human thought and social infidelity will seek to penetrate and ravage its bulwarked façade, and offers trust to no one.

Science scans relentlessly for Opportunity: beyond every forward step in understanding is another; beyond every exciting discovery is one more exciting still. The quest for the advancement of both is endless.

Science clings to Uniformity: the status quo in human knowledge is firmly fixed, more stubborn and entrenched than even the deepest bigotries and most nourished prejudices – it will only move when the strongest, most tested, most compelling of natural testimonies present; and even then, will only relent when those testimonies are generally accepted.

Science strives for Novelty: no other enterprise is as welcoming of diverse thought and unique perspective, for no other enterprise is as free of proclivity and penchant. Indeed, while it is the steady rain-drip of modest revelations that mark its quotidian march, it is the daring, fresh, unanticipated inquiry that tumbles paradigms.

In short, Science leans not one direction or another, within the frame of human cognition – it captures *all* of it.

For this reason, it is more complete, more functional - more *trustworthy* – than any of us, or any of our social institutions can ever be. It embraces every human trait that matters in our quest to survive and thrive.

Science – for all its emotional detachment, objective posture and political indifference - is the fullest, most complete expression of humanity.

The Low-Empathy Cognitive Cluster

This is happening in my neck of the woods (Central Kentucky, USA), where the governor is an Authoritarian carpet-bagger who blew into town (and into state office) just before election of Trump. He is widely hated for his assault on public education in the state.

Friends of mine elsewhere are taking him to task for this, calling him an asshole, etc., but the final point is this:

Matt Bevin's comments reveal a natural deficit of empathy, and that is common to his political party: disinterest in helping others-not-like-me, coupled with great interest in supporting others-like-me, derives from a sharp limitation in range of emotion for other human beings. This is evident in Bevin's party, not only today, but throughout history, and across cultures - "Right-wing" politics and social frames emit a disdain for Others, which is (mathematically) the same thing as constraint of empathy.

What this results in, when such people get together and form a political party/church/Facebook group is - wait for it! - a cognitive cluster. In other words, individual low empathy is reinforced by the social group, making its expression worse and worse.

And this is where I lose you all: *this is natural.* Empathy emanates from a region in the brain, the insular cortex; some of us are born with lots of tissue in this region, some with very little. Sociopaths have almost none at all.

My point: we can despise the products of expressions like Bevin's below, but we cannot despise Bevin himself for having this trait, any more than we can despise a gay man for his love of males or a black woman for her color or gender. They are *all* born that way.

What can we do instead?

We can calmly vote him out, and resolve to understand that high public office in a democratic system is not the best place for a low-empathy Authoritarian.

It's not a matter of opinion. Empathy emanates from the insular cortex, and some of us are born with lots of tissue in that region, some with very little. What we call a "sociopath" is someone with almost none. This is pure genetics. We can (and should) no more hate a person born this way that we would hate a black woman or a gay man. (As recently as 30 years ago, it was conventional in law enforcement to treat sociopathic crime as a pathology, not a moral wrong.)

All of that said, the expression of low empathy is socially driven. The natural low-empathy individual is either constrained or emboldened by the level of self-expression blessed by the group. Lately, the low-empathy crowd has been emboldened, such that it is in vogue to let fly with one's low-empathy impulses; in the past, not so much.

Similarly, when a low-empathy individual is surrounded by a high-empathy group (like Sheldon on "Big Bang Theory"), the low-empathy individual tends to rein in their low-empathy impulses.

Human Nature, Yet Again

We base our judgments of self and others upon our understanding of human nature, our subjective perception of what a human being is, how we function, how we grow and change. And it is not a surprise to anyone that human beings tend to group themselves according to this particular piece of worldview.

Our assumptions about human nature, however, are almost always (and should be) suspect, for the sources of this viewpoint are likewise suspect. A partial summary of where we get our ideas about human nature include our (equally subjective and tainted) parents and family members, peers, ancient holy books, media, and various educational systems - all of which serve only to perpetuate, and even amplify, existing flaws in our understanding.

The horror of this circumstance is that these competing views of human nature are all necessarily tainted and incorrect, and no sound basis for the establishment of social policy for the common good. No one religion can deliver universal peace and well-being; no one ideology can truly be good for all; no one economic viewpoint can establish a satisfying outcome for all participants. *All* of these systems of thought and behavior are based on specific and subjective (and inflexible) ideas about what a human being really is.

All of this can change, if we agree to rethink our social structures in the light of an objective account of human nature, one that recognizes and addresses the reality of human thought and emotion and group behaviors without the subjective (and often selfish) assumptions of religion and ideology and personal bias. Only one path leads us there - Science - and, well, science is hard work.

But hard work should not deter us. We built the pyramids. We landed on the moon. We conquered smallpox and polio. And all of those things were hard.

An objective, real account of human nature, free of subjective assumption and emotional shadows, would be a path to growth and universal prosperity unequaled in all of time and history and human thought...

It's Not...

It's not your 'platform' (which appears to have no planks at all); it's not your 'ideology,' which is self-contradictory in about 50 different ways; it's not your vision for the nation or your addiction to fear, bigotry, misogyny and inequality, your inability to cope with math and science or your need to inject your religion into absolutely everything.

It's your distorted, craven ideas about human nature that make you dangerous, your twisted idea of what human beings are, how we should treat each other and how you measure value in other people than makes me want you kept from power...

A Good Argument

A good argument...

- reveals the author; it is measured by the completeness of its transparency, the clarity of its values, the competence of its author, and its willingness to be vulnerable;

- must respect *every* reader/listener it encounters;

- must make a positive emotional connection with its recipient, beyond its intellectual efficacy; it must resonate with the readers 'sense of rightness', on the assumption that no reader measures 'rightness' in purely empirical terms;

- must appeal to humanity, not a cognitive cluster, lest it emerge a mere tract;

- must transcend agenda; the worthy argument is the courier of truth, in the service of knowledge and progress, rather than dominance or gain;

- defines its author; our quality of argument is our most earnest and complete CV;

- *teaches* argument; competent, persuasive, earnest argument is its own justification, and informs the reader as much through its style and construction as its evidence and reason;

- combines substance of thought with substance of feeling, bound by consistency;

- strives to be as complete as possible in the moment, while being unafraid to be tentative in the long run.

A good argument is our finest personal portrait.

On the Beach

On the Beach is a chilling movie (and novel) about the end of the world - all the more chilling because there are no special effects, no big moments, no high drama... just the final ticks of the human clock.

A nuclear war has already occurred as the film opens. The northern hemisphere and most of the southern are too radioactive for life to exist anymore. Everyone is dead. But the radiation has not yet reached Australia, where a pocket of humanity persists in comfort. But this, too, will end, as the winds will bring the radioactivity down under in less than six months.

The plot centers around a US submarine that does a final patrol, traveling from Australia back to San Francisco, gathering readings and confirming what they already know. Scenes of a completely empty city are more chilling than any big-budget visions of apocalypse; an AWOL sailor's cavalier assurance that he has 200 abandoned drugstores at his disposal for a quick suicide is almost perversely casual.

That's it, there's nothing more: just two hours of the last humans wrapping up their conflicted thoughts and trying to find a way to face not only their own ending, but the ending of all things.

This was hard enough to ponder during the Cold War; pondering it today, when the threat of annihilation emerges not from conflicting political ideologies, but from the craven self-interest of oligarchs, is downright brutal...

Heaven and Angels

We live highly compromised lives, within a social frame not meant for minds like ours.

That being the case, we cannot expose our deep selves to everyone - we are vulnerable, socially and emotionally, in ways our brains are not equipped to handle. We must be absurdly cautious of whom we allow into our private lives.

In the very distant past, the people around us were *all* intimates; we all lived and died together. We *all* had each other's backs. That is no longer true; and we must be wary of trusting those who might not be there when we need them.

I believe in a world to come, a near future, when this is no longer true - when human beings fully realize the miracle that they are, and appreciate *every* other human being as an equal miracle, deserving of absolute respect. In that world, we need no longer fear making ourselves vulnerable to others - because those others will respect and honor our vulnerability.

Earth is, in all the universe we can see, the closest thing to Heaven; humankind is, in all the universe we can see, the closest thing to angels.

WestWingWorld

Welcome to WestWingWorld, the ultimate Delos adult theme park! This unprecedented blending of state-of-the-art artificial intelligence, engineering, and dramatic innovation has created an astonishing world-within-a-world, a place where the discerning vacationer may be lost in a reverie of intellectual and philosophical extravagance, intimately celebrating the Washington of Aaron Sorkin in the company of hundreds of androids - "hosts", they are called – so life-like as to be indistinguishable from the other guests!

How does that sound? Who wouldn't want to be part of the Bartlet White House, if only for a few days – battling an opposition Congress, girded in social righteousness, surrounded by colleagues like Chief of Staff Leo McGarry, Deputy Chief Josh Lyman, Communications Director Toby Zieglar, Press Secretary C.J. Cregg, and Domestic Policy Advisor Sam Seaborn?

...To say nothing of the man himself, Jed Bartlet, First Lady Abby Bartlet, the First Daughters, body man Charlie Young, Mrs. Landingham, and the endless cast of supporting players that follow?

Who wouldn't want to relive, up close, the Mendoza Appointment? The Haffley Shutdown? The Santos Campaign? Who wouldn't want to be in the Oval Office for the Death Tax Elimination Act Veto, or Speaker Walken's swearing-in? In the Situation Room for Operation Swift Fury? In the Senate Chamber for the Stackhouse Filibuster? In the National Cathedral for Bartlet's rant against the Almighty after Mrs. Landingham's funeral?

WestWingWorld offers all of this and more! The characters of *The West Wing* come to life in full-scale replicas of the White House, the Mall, Capitol Hill and select sections of Georgetown. More than 140 narratives are available; for those who know all the words of every episode, it's possible to step into the role of any major character, including the president – or you can participate improvisationally as an extra, adding your own accents to Sorkin's beloved stories.

Have you ever dreamed of being Presidents Carter, Clinton and JFK all rolled into one? Then be Josiah Barlet, Nobel Prize-winning ex-governor of New Hampshire, the shortest president since Truman – brilliant, yet accessible; erudite, yet folksy – and try out that Oval Office chair! Get Roberto Mendoza confirmed to the Supreme Court! Holler for Mrs. Landingham! Refuse Toby's resignations! Broker peace between Israel and Palestine! Fail to disclose your multiple sclerosis! All in a day's work.

Or be the president's best friend, the ultra-competent Leo: run the country, inspire your staff, urge the president to roll up his sleeves! Yank the vice president's chain! Endure public humiliation over your past substance abuse; dance with women six inches taller than you; square off against Lord John Marbury; admonish the Religious Right! Get taken out for a walk by a Congressional committee! Relive your heart attack in the Birnam Woods!

Are you dour, joyless, self-righteous, and even smarter than the president himself? Then you'll enjoy being Toby Zieglar, identifying Walter Hufnagle's overcoat on the Mall; refusing pie from ex-wife Andy by the Potomac, or providing her with sperm for in vitro fertilization; getting up in the president's face, oh, just about any time; or leaking the existence of a classified military space shuttle to Greg Brock of the *New York Times*. Or just save social security!

What woman wouldn't love to be C.J. Gregg for a while? Be the press secretary presidents dream of! Be wittier and quicker on your feet than the entire White House press corps combined; tease Danny Concannon; be stunning in off-the-rack dresses; be *really great* in bed! Then step into the role of Chief of Staff, under the worst of circumstances, leapfrogging all of your male colleagues, without missing a beat!

If you're too arrogant to live and too sexy for your shirt, you'll do well as Josh Lyman – Leo's right hand, supervisor of 1,100 West Wing staffers, and the 101st senator. Bring home the Family Wellness Act; steal the First Lady's $12 million immunization education fund; thwart your activist girlfriend Amy by hiring her boss; take a bullet in the chest and come up swinging! Or work his other side, and diss Mary Marsh on national television; lean on Senator Carrick so hard that he turns Republican; take Donna for granted until she quits and joins the Russell campaign.

And how 'bout that Donna, right? You could *be* her, fighting the good fight alongside Josh every day, building up the know-how and skills that will eventually make *you* a chief of staff yourself, to the next FLOTUS! Live it all, from your brazen on-boarding in the first campaign, to your missile-silo-under-the-Eisenhower-putting-green gaffe, to the Gaza mission and your near-death in the suburban - and your bittersweet moments with Irish photojournalist Colin Ayres.

And if you're cool as all hell but don't need to flaunt it, you'll do well as Charlie Young, the president's body man – smarter than Josh and Sam and C.J. put together, loved like a son by the president (don't miss the Paul Revere's Knife Scene!), and loved like a lover by his youngest daughter. You'll wake the president at ungodly hours; watch for symptoms of M.S.; bust Zoey's sexual harassers in a Georgetown bar; have the president himself do your tax return! Proudly refuse immunity in the M.S. cover-up investigation - or experience the existential horror of realizing that it was you, not the president, that the shooters at Roslyn were gunning for.

And, of course, it wouldn't be the West Wing without Sam. You can be the earnest, talented deputy communications director, outshining even the president in your optimism, balancing out that moody Toby with your youthful pluck and constant good spirits. Land the State of the Union! Spar with Ainsley Hayes! Walk out of Gage Whitney on the spur of the moment, just from a glance at Josh's bad poker face; sit with Nancy McNally in the Sit Room, defending Daniel Galt; leak the Ritchie campaign's nasty opposition video by mistake, jeopardizing your boss's re-elect; run for Congress to comfort a hometown widow!

It's not just the characters that make WestWingWorld special; it's the unique experience of living among androids that look and feel and act as real as you yourself.

Are you action-oriented? Do bombs, bullets and mayhem get your engine running? Well, that's no problem, because the hosts of WestWingWorld are just machines – you aren't breaking any laws or truly committing any moral breach! You won't *really* be assassinating Abdul Sharif; you won't *really* be blowing up four high-rated military targets in Syria; when you blow away the shooters in the window at Roslyn, they won't *really* die!

And think of the off-script possibilities: wouldn't it be great to be Secret Service agent Simon Donovan, walk into that convenience store and, instead of being killed, take down both robbers, then do C.J. all night long?

Yes, if you've got some mojo that needs indulging, WestWingWorld hosts are *fully functional*, able to cater to the most intimate desires of guests – completely consequence-free, because they're just robots! You can be Sam, and accidentally sleep with a prostitute; be the First Lady, and take the president's temperature "recreationally"; experience a night of shame with the philandering John Hoynes; step out of Charlie Young's shoes, and into First Daughter Zoey's bedroom after hours (or vice versa), right under the president's nose!

Or change *West Wing* history in this domain as well – be Josh, having a campaign fling with Donna on the first campaign, rather than the last; or be Sam, and get it on with Leo's daughter Mallory at the Kennedy Center; be C.J., and decide you no longer have a problem with the press secretary dating a reporter.

Just $40,000 a day is all it takes to bring the imaginary world of Aaron Sorkin's *West Wing* to life – to experience the living, breathing characters we've all loved these many years, to make yourself part of the action! Call or visit our website today, and get started on the greatest, most mentally stimulating vacation of your life!

UPDATE: WestWingWorld will be closing indefinitely, pending extensive review and revision of its revenue model. Due to numerous media revelations of the recent string of guest bankruptcies, foreclosures, exorbitant credit card debt and exhausted retirement accounts, a number of fraud investigations at both federal and state levels have been initiated.

Park administrators have assured the public and press that no malfeasance has occurred, that many guests truly have been spending all that they have, free of coercion or undue influence, to continue being in the park, and have issued the following statement from the Delos public relations office:

"WestWingWorld's inquiry into the recent financial difficulties of its most frequent guests has included extensive exit surveys, compiling their reactions to the narratives in which they have participated. The conclusion of our counselors, as well as outside consultants, is uniform: once guests experience truly good government, immersed in a world of competent, intelligent, committed and principled public servants who forego more comfortable and lucrative lives in order to do some real good – a world where they truly matter, and the greater good ultimately prevails over craven politics and the cynicism of partisanship - they simply cannot bring themselves to ever leave."

The Problem

People who wish to live within a social hierarchy tend to cluster into groups, and to consider those who do not to be a danger.

People who wish to live within a social structure of equality tend to cluster into groups, and to consider those who do not to be a danger.

People who are highly sensitive to threat tend to cluster into groups, and to consider those who do not to be a danger.

People who are highly sensitive to opportunity tend to cluster into groups, and to consider those who do not to be a danger.

People who find satisfaction in the known and familiar tend to cluster into groups, and to consider those who do not to be a danger.

People who find satisfaction in exploring and seeking out the new and different tend to cluster into groups, and to consider those who do not to be a danger.

Each of us born with a natural predisposition to some combination of these tendencies, and to live our lives accordingly.

It is not the tendencies that are the problems; that our species has so many circulating within our genes is our salvation.

It is the groups that are the problem. They explain almost everything that's wrong with us.

Fullness of Consciousness, Bonds of Strange Loops

Let's briefly revisit our Paleo past.

We know lots about who we used to be, from the traces of ancient living our ancestors left behind and scrutiny of genes they passed on to us. We know that they lived together, died together, and were generally closer than what we call 'family' today. We know these clans numbered between 100 and 150, seldom smaller, never more. We know that they shared our diversity of thought, and used it to their advantage, and that many of the pressures we impose upon our kind today could not have existed then.

Flash forward to the present. Cognitive scientist/philosopher Douglas Hofstadter presents us with an idea of formidable explanatory power and stunning elegance – that bits and pieces of our "selves" (he calls them 'strange loops') get passed between us, when we are intimately close to someone else, when we share every day and most experiences. In the modern world, that would include marriage partners, parents and children, best friends, etc.

We can easily self-examine and see that there's something to what Hofstadter is saying: certainly our own worldviews are gentled into change through years of living and loving closely, and certainly we all have that handful of special people in our past who brought us around to a new way of thinking, an enhanced perspective.

The thing is...

In the Paleolithic past, that list of people with whom we exchanged bits and pieces of our inner strange loops would have been *most of the people in our clan.*

Think about that!

If Hofstadter is right – and if our portrait of our Paleo predecessors is correct – then human consciousness as it was once experienced is now extinct. We only open ourselves intimately to a comparatively scant range of others, compared to our ancestors, and thus only absorb scant strange loop bits and pieces. We are left to our own dank inner echoes for the majority of our personal development.

What does this say about the world we've created? Can it be that we are needlessly truncating most of what we could fully be, if we were as socially open and immersive and integrated as our ancestors?

And can we do something about that?

Two Worlds

Each of us lives in two worlds: the actual physical world that exists whether we're here or not, and the world each of us carries around in our head, which only exists there, only for the individual toting it around.

The word for the one in our heads is 'model' - we each experience our existence in the physical world and build a model of it in our brains, a model that contains bits and pieces of the real one but which can never be complete. We need this model to survive, to store memories, to make plans, to anticipate the future. We couldn't exist without it; our personal model of reality is what empowers us to make the most of reality.

But our models of the world are private, individual, unique: no two are the same. Yet every single world-model hosted by a human mind contributes to others, and receives contributions in turn.

The actual world is only affected by these virtual worlds to the extent that human beings impact it by living in it (minimally in the past, profoundly today).

There's just one problem.

The modeled world within the brain evolved to support survival in the real world. It is, in effect, a working log of truths about the real world that serve the objective of living in it. Put simply, when the real world changed - or when a new truth about the real world presented itself - the modeled world in the mind of a person living in it would absorb that new information and modify the world-model in their brain. That has worked splendidly for hundreds of thousands of years.

Today, our survival is a given - and truth about the world, upon which survival once depended, is no longer essential; it can even be (and has been) repurposed.

Today, it's no longer necessary to keep the world-model in our minds in sync with the real one; we'll live a long and comfortable life whether we stay in sync or not. Today, we don't even walk the Earth enough to even fully experience or gather information about it first-hand.

Worse, we no longer modify the world-model in our minds to match reality; we modify the representation of reality to conform to the world-model in our minds.

While it's understandable how this situation came to be, it is nonetheless deeply troubling - and a catastrophic mistake for humankind. All that is good and useful and life-saving about the inexpressibly sacred gift of mind and self-awareness that we enjoy is muted and weakened by this reversal of what is real and what isn't.

The end result for the individual - living in their virtual world, rather than the real one - has terrible consequences both for them and for humankind as a whole, consequences that are all too blatant and obvious, today and throughout the recorded past; for living in the modeled world of the brain is living in an illusion - an incomplete, partially incorrect, ultimately unshareable illusion that is, at best, a distorted lens aimed at the actual world.

The consequences begin with false euphoria. We have isolated ourselves from the real ecstasies of our physical existence, the thrill of living in the most beautiful, exciting place in all of time and space, substituting cheap imitations of joy and satisfaction based on delusions and falsehoods. We no longer flourish as we once did; what sense of wonder we still indulge is at best a seasonal ritual.

The consequences continue with the shattering effect our world-models have on our unity as a species. Where once we lived and died together, loved and thrived and experienced the world together, now we huddle in our modeled realities in desperate fragmentation, even forfeiting our own modeled understandings to those of others - others who exploit our disunity to prop up their own distorted worlds. We once walked the world together, cherishing our lives; now we walk on one another, cherishing our modeled worlds. The cooperation that once fueled our world-models is faltering, and with it, our ability to care for our species as a whole.

And the greatest consequence, the one we won't even look at, threatens our continued existence: living with a preference for our modeled reality is slowly robbing us of our capacity to meet the challenges of actual reality. Our astonishing powers of mind and awareness, our ability to secure our existence in our unpredictable Eden, depends upon those things the real world offers when we are fully engaged with living in it, rather than loitering in our own heads - the truths the real world perpetually presents, to begin with; the essential vigor of perpetual change, along the way; and our honest experience of one another, most importantly.

Most shattering in consideration of this dysfunctional collective choice is that it IS a choice: there is nothing forcing us, as individuals, to choose our illusory inner realities over the bounty of actual reality; there is no conscious edict, no explicit imperative dictating how we choose to experience our lives. We are simply allowing ourselves to be seduced.

And we can, one person at a time, turn and look at the heaven we inhabit, and allow ourselves to be seduced by a more authentic song: we can fall in love with what is real, and allow ourselves to thrive again.

We'd better.

Empathy and Capitalism

Empathy is hard-wired into the human brain. It is a survival mechanism that is very rare in the animal kingdom in general, and uncommon even in higher mammals. It isn't a choice, it isn't a learned thing; it is built in - we roll off the factory floor with it.

That said, the amount of empathy experienced by any one individual often differs somewhat from that of any other; there is variability in how much empathy each of us feels.

More than that, it's not all about how much empathy we feel; it's as much about how much - and in what ways - society trains us to express it. Here, too, there is considerable variability.

Gary Olson addresses this in his excellent book *Empathy Imperiled: Capitalism, Culture, and the Brain.* His premise is that capitalism, by design, suppresses our natural hard-wired imperative to work together to survive. Empathy is the engine of cooperation, and we have used that engine to travel very far very quickly, in evolutionary terms.

Capitalism does damage in this domain on several levels, Olson asserts. To begin with, it is based on a set of presuppositions that are increasingly odds with the findings of neurophysiology, evolutionary anthropology and behavioral genetics: it assumes that human beings are naturally selfish, that our deep impulse is not cooperation but competition.

Here, Olson has a mountain to climb, for it is certainly true that we are immersed in examples of human selfishness daily, that we have all committed acts of selfishness at one time or another, and that selfishness is certainly the rule among many species other than our own. But he has the latest research on his side: the deeper we dive into our paleolithic roots, the clearer it becomes that cooperation, not competition, kept us alive through hundreds of thousands of years under predation. Moreover, the more we learn about the wiring of the human brain, the more we see 'cooperation circuits', rather than 'competition circuits'.

The disconnect, Olson demonstrates, is in the social structures we are born and raised in - capitalism being the most destructive of the lot. The background messages of capitalism are that we are all in competition with one another, that our personal mission is acquisition and that the ideal position in society is one of dominance. Moreover, he articulates, the member wishing to thrive must constantly be on guard, wary of others, alert for the possibility of deceit and exploitation, and reluctant to share.

These ideas, per Olson, are not innate but unnatural, created by the few to manipulate the many, and that capitalism as an expression of human nature is not only not constructive but toxic.

He quotes Joel Bakan: "As the corporation comes to dominate society - through, among other things, privatization and commercialization - its ideal conception of human nature becomes dominant, too. And it is a frightening prospect. The corporation, after all, is deliberately designed to be a psychopath: purely self-interested, incapable of concern for others, amoral and without conscience - in a word, inhuman - and its goal...is to ensure that the human beings who it is interacting with, you and me, also become inhuman."

There is, to be sure, nothing of the natural human to be found in the corporate citizen. It has more in common with the leopard and wolf, whose concerns never extend beyond self, and whose only goal is to feed. There is nothing of the communities of the veldt, whose members lived and loved and died as one, mastering the harshest of worlds with new ways, thriving and moving forward at astonishing pace through the simple mechanism of sharing everything with everyone.

All of that said, it is certainly true that not all competition is unhealthy, not all business bloodthirsty; that the act of negotiation is often the best mode of cooperation; that motivations matter. But gone are the days, Olson argues, when capitalists can claim the high ground in the march of social progress, or any ownership at all of the human profile. On the data, on the history, on the examples emerging around us, the lie is put to the textbook distortions of Adam Smith: the Invisible Hand, we are rediscovering, exists not to push, but to reach out...

My Partisan Friend

It was three years or so ago, maybe a little more, that my partisan friend tried to pin me to his office corkboard with one of the labels he finds so essential to organizing his world.

"Years ago, I took you for a conservative," he was saying; "You come from a conservative family, and most of our friends in common are from the church you were attending."

"It's true that I probably overstayed my welcome in church," I agreed, "but that's just inertia from my upbringing; I had very few social or political views in common with our church friends."

"And now it's pretty obvious you're a liberal, from the stuff you post in social media," he continued. "You're all about reducing inequality and regulating big business and that climate stuff."

"That's perfectly fair," I nodded, "and it's also true that I'm registered as a Democrat in the county where I live. But that's more to do with the fact that I live in a state where I can only vote in primaries if I'm registered as something. I wouldn't register as a Republican, but that's not a political choice."

"Well, then, are you a moderate? You're pro-regulation, but you also own a business, right? And you're all about globalism, but aren't you also in favor of a strong national defense?"

"All true, but I wouldn't call myself a moderate, either," I replied.

He was exasperated.

"If it's unclear, it's not your fault and it isn't my fault. It's because we don't define 'partisan' the same way."

This seemed to puzzle him.

"If I seem to lean left in my views, it's not because I'm a liberal; in fact, I'm fine with rejecting that label. I seem to lean left not because I embrace the Democratic Party, but because I embrace science."

(This was a year before Trump became president, and three years before his people said "Science is a Dem thing.")

"I don't think 'left' is good and 'right' is bad," I continued, "and I certainly don't think 'right' is good and 'left' is bad. I think the entire idea of 'left' and 'right', partisanism in general, is misguided and destructive.

"My views aren't 'liberal' or 'Democrat'; if they seem that way, it's luck of the draw. If I have social and political positions, they are derived from my understanding of science."

"-and liberals and Democrats are more accepting of science than Republicans and conservatives," my partisan friend said. "Doesn't that make you one of them?"

"I'm not accepting of science because liberals and Democrats accept science," I explained, "I'm accepting of liberals and Democrats because they are accepting of science. Do you see the difference? The bottom line for me is objective observation and study of the world, and evidence-based reasoning is the best path to good decision-making about public policy and social development."

"You're just substituting 'science' for 'party' - it's just a trick of language," my friend objected. "You're still in the same place, with regard to politics."

"I'm in good company, then," I replied. "Most of the Framers were against partisanism, and were men of science and reason. Call me a member of the Framers Party.

"I don't favor the policies and positions I do because liberals and Democrats like them," I continued. "I favor them because the data, the evidence, and history demonstrate that they work better. If the data and evidence on any position I hold were to support a Republican viewpoint, I would happily glow red on that position."

"I'm finding that hard to imagine," my friend said skeptically.

"I'm not surprised," I agreed. "But an example would be the ACA. The raw truth is that it was a compromise that served the goal of placing healthcare within the reach of every citizen by way of a market solution. You can call it Obamacare, but the truth is it was a Republican idea, one that was well-reasoned and had data behind it. It was worthy of support, as a step forward if not as a long-term solution. The politics surrounding it are distracting, immature nonsense, and I want to stand as far apart from that as possible.

"My point is that I don't care if you call it Obamacare or Romneycare, the left and right of it don't matter. What matters is that it was a good idea and I don't care which 'side' came up with it. I only care about the quality of the idea."

"I understand the point you're trying to make," my friend said, "but I don't see you getting very far in making it."

"Again, I don't care," I shrugged. "I'm okay with people not getting it. Like I said, we don't define 'partisan' the same way."

"Your way is a lot more work," my friend grinned. "Most people don't want to put that much effort into it."

"I know," I said, "but the alternative is to trade the appearance of being partisan for actually *being* partisan. And I don't think I could handle that kind of stress."

By Accident of Birth

Things you received by accident of birth, for which you bear no blame and deserve no credit:

You received your gender by accident of birth.

Your hair color is by accident of birth.

Your adult height is by accident of birth.

Your skin color is by accident of birth.

Your sexual orientation is by accident of birth.

But that's not all...

Your nationality is by accident of birth.

Your religion is by accident of birth.

The love you received (or not) from your parents is by accident of birth.

Your cognitive type - your worldview - is by accident of birth.

Put another way – *no one* is born "deserving," for better or worse, the hand they are dealt by birth; and if that is true, then *everyone* is worthy of your compassion.

The Digital Capitalist

What is the true value of a human being?

The value assigned to a person depends, almost inevitably, upon the group they belong to. Our worth is established by our tribe.

We see this as a human constant: it happens in the most complex modern society; it happens in the most primitive tribe. We see it in our ancient texts, our folklore, we see it in the products of scientific inquiry. A human being is as valuable as the tribe allows.

The result is a staggering range of value: in some cultures, human life in general is not particularly prized; in others, all human life is sacrosanct. More often, the rule is that Some People are Worth More Than Others, and the criteria by which this worth is measured can be just about anything.

We see that even in modern times, when Science leaves us no excuse, that those who are not the same color as the majority are of lesser worth; we see that those who do not possess the same gender as that of the ruling class are not as valued.

And in modern societies based on capitalism, where material prosperity and the capacity to increase it are all, those who possess more material wealth are themselves considered to be of greater human value than those with less.

And finally, there is an insoluble paradox: those who produce a great deal are of greater human value than those who do not - yet those who engage in actual material production (that is, those who work in factories, on farms, etc.) are of lesser worth than those who collect the wealth that derives from their efforts.

And the even greater paradox: among the most primitive surviving hunter-gatherer tribes, the individual is assigned greater value, regardless of role, than the worth granted the individual who does not contribute to capitalist imperatives in the material society.

It is rightly pointed out that capitalist disdain for those who do not devote themselves to increasing the wealth of the ruling class is not at all an American innovation, but a British import: London was the pacesetter in this deeply toxic world view - but America has taken it to new heights.

An individual's perceived worth is a function of how much they earn, how valued their trade or profession is, and their commitment to the system.

But now...

Just as robots have been replacing human workers in factories, diminishing their production value, we now have the same thing happening in the office: AI is rapidly growing more sophisticated, able to absorb increasing swaths of white-collar functionality with greater speed, efficiency and accuracy than humans can achieve - at far lower cost.

In short, the disdain of the upper-class capitalist for the unproductive worker necessarily grows, as technology continues to encroach upon - and enrich - society.

But wait...

It doesn't take a master's in mathematics to note that the vector of that change is headed straight for the upper-class capitalist himself.

At first, technology was simply replacing human labor. That's been happening since the invention of the wheel.

Then technology stepped into the role of accomplishing repetitive soft tasks - simple cause-and-effect chores and routine math work (which computers do far faster and more accurately than human beings do anyway).

But technology can't make big decisions! Technology can't innovate! Technology can't be creative! (all traits that the upper-class capitalist ascribes to self).

It can't replace what makes human beings unique and special!

Technology couldn't... until now.

Artificial Intelligence isn't simply computer power applied to human problems; it's the best of human decision-making power supercharged with a billion-fold increase in speed and accuracy, supplemented with access to far more data than the human mind can absorb.

Not creative? Tell that to AlphaGo Zero, a gaming system that defeated not only every human champion but all of its digital peers, by inventing new strategies no human mind had ever conceived.

In short, computers are already powerful enough, intelligent enough and creative enough to begin tackling problems far greater than calendar management and warehouse inventories and truck deliveries: it is entering the realm of configuring new synthetic molecules for pharmaceutical needs; reconfiguring virtual communications infrastructure on the fly, to increase human connectivity in a constantly-changing world; and learning more from observing human behavior than we are able to learn on our own.

Put another way, we are approaching a time when an AI can run a multi-national corporation, manage a national economy, monitor a national defense and coordinate international relations more efficiently than even the best and most gifted human beings.

Where, then, is human value?

If the super-wealthy no longer have their wealth as justification of their worth, what happens to their contention that wealth and productivity are measures of human worth?

What happens to "Each according to his contribution" when machines are doing all the contributing (and, we have to point out, meeting all our needs)?

If material production is no longer the yardstick of a person's value, what will be that yardstick now?

If the process of meeting the material needs of human needs, and thus ensuring human survival, is no longer in the hands of human beings - then don't we need another means of assigning worth to people?

Of course we do.

We will have to seek measures of human value in human behavior - not in the production of food and clothing and shelter and safety, but in the creation of their byproducts: health and happiness and community; art and music and ideas; exploration and adventure and discovery.

Joy.

The argument can be made that capitalism has contributed to the availability of all these things, with the possible exception of joy; but capitalism was never necessary to their existence.

And if you doubt that - just ask the Native Americans...

Universal Trust

Continuing our discussion of the concept of trust, having visited Azim Shariff's notions that the invention of religion was specifically an innovative expression of trust, we can ask ourselves: if we can't know everyone around us intimately enough to trust them naturally, and if trust based on religious identity is easily faked - what, then, can we trust in?

We have an answer to that, and we've had it for a while now. We just need to learn how to apply it.

Trust cultivates the belief that we are hearing the truth from another. Trust is the assurance that a result is honest. Trust is having our expectations rewarded with outcomes that can be reliably anticipated.

Trust is what evolved over the countless millennia during which we relied on the honest report of our community fellows; were able to accept what happens next because what we were told came from those with more experience; made great strides in cooperation that kept us alive and well-fed and growing, developing at a pace unprecedented, because we were able to act as one - because we trusted one another.

What can we trust?

We apply trust to knowledge, to the experience of others, to expectations of behavior. When we intimately know and understand those we are called upon to trust, this is easy to do. What is needed is a system for conveying knowledge, for evaluating the experience of others, and for testing expectations.

What would that system need to be?

It would need to be divorced from any single human arbiter: if it was to apply universally, it would have to represent everyone, and thus not be tied to anyone. It would need to be objective.

Knowledge derived from my own experience passes all my personal tests for it; knowledge that could be universally trusted would have to pass everyone's personal tests.

Those tests, then, would have to be rigorously applied - only the knowledge that did so would then be trusted.

Knowledge derived from my own experience must be consistent with my prior experience; it would have to fit into my model of the world, in order to be trusted.

Universal knowledge would likewise have to be consistent with what is already known, fitting into an objective model of the world, in order to be trusted.

We have this way of knowing, this system of establishing trust, already. We call it Science, and it's been around for many decades. It gives us a way of testing what we know, what we accept, and - if we are in earnest - determining what is worthy of offering to others.

Is it perfect? No. But it's far better, far harder to fool, by orders of magnitude, than religious trust.

Is it as good as subjective personal trust? That's a tough one; we don't yet have a way to know that, because we have no easy way to test what modern humans would do, and how well they would behave, in a scenario where they lived their entire lives among a mere 100 people, under modern conditions.

And if we did know, how would we go about implementing it?

I would argue that we're already on our way. Many professions, not just Science, have implemented (albeit imperfectly) similar standards of trust. Law, Medicine, Journalism - what we now call the 'fact-based professions'. Adherence to evidence, reason, structured discourse and high performance standards is, at least, an aspiration.

We can build that adherence into additional professions as we march forward - into public service, technology, education - rewarding those innovators who take those professions in a fact-based direction. We are already turning to tech to make business and government 'data-driven' - and that's a start.

And we can make a personal commitment to rethink trust in objective, empirical terms, to take in that knowledge and expectation that have a basis in provable fact, giving less weight to offerings that don't - and testing the success or failure of the trust we grant against the outcomes. That's harder work - but it takes us to a better place.

For Religion to Work...

Religion only works if its adherents 1) surrender their cognitive independence; 2) outsource their personal decision-making (and responsibility for it) to their religious authorities, and 3) replace their own sense of right/wrong behavior with the group's prevailing defaults.

To achieve this, the adherent must steer clear of authorities beyond the group; avoid new information that contradicts that provided by the group's leaders; and decline to interact meaningfully with persons not in the group, whose behavior does not conform to the group's default behaviors. Otherwise, the religion becomes unsustainable.

Whatever Father Says

For over two years now, since Donald Trump took the GOP nomination for president, the rest of the world has been watching, waiting, and asking, "How far is *too* far?"

There has been a passive belief – hope, really – within the punditry, within the media, within the dwindling ranks of traditional Republicans, and among America's breathless allies that Trump will eventually do something so outlandish, deceitful or treacherous that his base will fall away.

And as Trump grows more outlandish, more deceitful and more treacherous with each news cycle, we are beginning to see that such a day is never coming.

Trump himself famously declared, in an Iowa campaign rally in 2016, that "I could stand in the middle of 5th Avenue and shoot somebody and I wouldn't lose voters."

And he's absolutely right.

There is no behavior so outlandish that his true believers will bail on him. There is no gaucherie, no moral transgression, no betrayal too severe. Whatever Trump does, and whomever he does it to, he will forever remain righteous and unassailable in the eyes of his ever-loyal base.

He can lie with impunity. He can indulge in all manner of sexual depravity and remain pure. He can set fire to our alliances, our economy, our most cherished traditions and institutions, our very way of life - and yet be seen as a builder, not a destroyer. He truly could shoot somebody in the middle of 5th Avenue and not lose them.

And – most bizarre of all! - his most loyal, imperturbable fans in his base are Evangelical Christians, the supposed guardians of morality, who after decades of punctilious parading over the most tenuous indiscretions of public figures not in their fold are now turning two blind eyes to all of Trump's vulgarity, philandering, bigotry, dishonesty, and turpitude.

How can this be?

Though it eludes understanding and confounds all reason, this isn't really that hard to understand; it isn't even new. What we see in the Trump base is what we have *always* seen in the nature of the Authoritarian follower. The past two years are only the latest in a long parade of leader-follower dynamics among Authoritarians.

Cognitive scientist George Lakoff is a pacesetter in the field, explaining what he calls S*trict Father Morality*, an emotional predisposition in the Authoritarian mind:

"You have God above Man... you have Man above Nature, we can take anything we want for our use – you have the strong above the weak – that hierarchy follows, from one idea: it's Strict Father Morality applied to all aspects of life. That is what Trump not only believes, but acts on and assumes is correct – and he knows that about 35 percent of the country, the 35 percent who still support him also believe this, even if they're poor.

"The main thing is, if that is your worldview, and that's your morality, that defines who you are as a person; it's self-definition. And people don't vote against their self-definition. Not only that, it doesn't matter if Trump lies to them, and they know he's lying, because there's a higher truth – which is Strict Father Morality *itself*, which has consequences, and they are truer than any lies – and that if you deny that, if you accept the lies as more important, you're denying your self-identity."

Put another way: in the eyes of his true believers, Trump cannot break the law, because Trump *is* the law; he cannot be immoral, because he is the *embodiment* of moral; he cannot lie, he is always right, *because he is the truth*.

Whatever Trump says goes, no matter the contradictions, no matter the consequences.

Okay, Lakoff gives us a definition of the dynamic we're seeing, and it is enough to fine-tune our expectations. But it doesn't contain a why – what makes a person an Authoritarian Follower?

Now we hear from Erich Fromm, who foresaw the Authoritarian dynamic that emerged in Germany in the days of World War II:

"The function of an Authoritarian ideology and practice can be compared to the function of neurotic symptoms," he wrote in his seminal tome *Escape from Freedom.* "Such symptoms result from unbearable psychological conditions, and at the same time, offer a solution that makes life possible; yet they are not a solution that leads to happiness or growth of personality. They leave unchanged the conditions that necessitate the neurotic solution.

"Those who join the ranks of an Authoritarian cause to resolve inner turmoil and self-doubt are always its most fervent, rigidly ideological and loyal members. They are often its most politically influential members, as well."

President Dwight Eisenhower, writing to a dying veteran, framed the Authoritarian dynamic this way:

"The mental stress and burden that animates [Authoritarian] movements is admonition to beware the danger posed to democracy by those who seek freedom from the necessity of informing themselves and making up their own minds concerning... tremendous, complex and difficult questions."

The Authoritarian Follower is subconsciously seeking relief from deep, unexamined anxieties, and finding that relief in the Strict Father's dominance; s/he is made to feel safe and secure by Father's aggressive rhetoric, and is paradoxically made to feel stronger within the safe confines of Father's beneficent asylum.

All Trump had to do to win his base's loyalty was tap into that - to fan the flames of their fears, to despise the same institutions they despise, to hate the same people they hate; to make them feel more like *themselves* than they feel in the raucous pell-mell of the messy, uncertain, multicultural milieu of their homeland's democracy.

And that explains the next piece of the Authoritarian puzzle: it's not really about Trump. *Any* Social Dominator will do; *any* 'Strict Father' is perfectly acceptable to the Authoritarian Follower, as long as identity is validated, fear is assuaged, and comforting animosities are justified.

"I swear to you," Ronald Reagan, Jr. said to journalist Chris Matthews, "that if it were left just up to Donald Trump's base, they would elect Vladimir Putin as president of the United States over virtually anybody with a 'D' after their name."

And that's no exaggeration.

No sin is too great. No outrage too obscene. No leader is too despotic, no morality too inviolate. The Authoritarian Follower is a prisoner is his own mind, an inescapable stockade not of his own making, from which there is no escape. There is no recourse, other than to deflect the ascent of those who would rise high enough on the public landscape to harness them.

Arguing with them is pointless; they cannot speak our language. Hating them is folly; it only gives them strength. And disenfranchising them is hypocrisy; it hastens the spread of the poison that consumes them.

They are who they are.

"The lust for power is not rooted in strength, but in weakness; it is the expression of the individual self to stand alone and live. It is the desperate attempt to gain secondary strength where genuine strength is lacking." ~Fromm

Levers of the Mind

The levers of the human mind are so easily moved by other humans as to make it almost inconceivable that cooperation is not our default state. We submit readily to the perpetual influence of those around us, receptive to their emotions and actions and ideas, with no trace of the inherent aggression and independence and isolation of other mammals.

Generation Z, Part II

Earlier, I posted a short essay about a conversation I had with my teenage daughter about how her generation - Z - seems to differ from the preceding generations more radically and significantly than any such gap seen in living memory.

She agreed, and her answer to how that came to be is that she and her peers were the first generation raised entirely in the Internet. That's true, and in hindsight it's easy to see a lengthy array of unintended consequences.

We discussed how this early and constant exposure to the Internet gave her generation an earlier and deeper model of the world in their heads, built on norms that seem astonishingly out of sync with the models we had 40 years ago. So many things my generation took for granted have slipped away, and her generation cannot conceive of them - civility in public discourse, for instance - let alone miss them.

Another consequence she called out took my breath away. She noted that in TV, movies and books, she sees young people suffering from broken self-esteem, because they received insufficient validation from those around them. I have family members who experienced this, and she (and her friends) have seen it in relatives only moderately older than they are.

But that's not so much a problem for Gen Z, she informed me. She and her generation were born into a reality that places endless communities of sympathetic peers at their fingertips. When one of them feels alone, misunderstood, unsupported or otherwise alienated, it's the work of a minute to get on the Internet and seek out like-minded friends-to-be.

"We've known since we were small that we never have to feel alone," she told me.

Think about that!!!

I've been an online community member since long before Facebook - almost 20 years, now that I think about it - and *even now* it never occurs to me that I can always seek out friendly faces and understanding listeners with a few quick clicks.

The irony here is that I, of all people, should have realized this truth of the Internet right up front. I was raised in astounding isolation, a member of an almost cult-like Fundamentalist religion that kept my entire family largely disconnected from the world. We were actually at church 4-6 times a week; all vacations were with other church families; spring breaks and summer vacations included religious camp and other church-based training. There was no "outside world" that we could really reach, no external opinions or ideas, at least not until I reached high school.

I sit here now, remembering those days, and imagine how different my life would have been if I could have sought out kids like me online, back in my childhood.

To be sure, such online enclaves can offer danger as well as comfort; we have noted here many times that too much like-mindedness is both personally and socially destructive. But the idea that company and comfort and inclusion is now truly that easy to achieve is something that isn't obvious, goes unpondered, yet is utterly game-changing, as a spark of social evolution.

And there sits my daughter, sipping her iced tea, utterly taking it for granted; my teenage daughter, whose reality it is that despite whatever insecurities of youth gnaw at her, she need never feel alone.

Is it any wonder we see a teenage nation rising that is like no other? When the Boomers and Gen X have passed - all too soon! - the kind of solitude and isolation that factored huge in our own sense of who we were will vanish from the social gestalt. It also portends a return of humankind to an earlier, better state - a state of social integration that side-steps our ubiquitous class nonsense and imaginary barriers, all the machinations of centuries that have separated us and herded us and fooled us into believing we were people we really weren't. Gen Z has known since the dawning of awareness that when they can't count on the people around them, community is only a click or two away.

It's not that simple, of course; those terrible barriers and machineries that keep us divided have been hauled into our online experience, where they operate even more shamelessly than they do in meatspace; but Gen Z is all too casual - more so than we! - in their understanding that when their validation is threatened, it can be protected with the simple pressing of a Delete key.

Again, I had no words to offer my daughter as these truths spilled out of her. Again, I felt shame at the shabby world we're leaving to them, as well as a chill at the thought of how coldly practical Gen Z has already become.

But most chilling of all is the squandered opportunity of the reality she is sharing with me: her generation and mine now have the tools to correct thousands of years of malfeasance in the construction of social reality...

...but we don't have the will to do it.

Toxic

The Left says the Right is toxic. The Right says the Left is toxic.

Both are correct.

Partisanism is toxic.

Cognitive clusters are toxic.

Self-isolating groups are toxic.

Any social collective that out-selects those who think differently is toxic: it is a place where cortical processing atrophies and self-destructive mantras take root; it is a place where some human beings must be diminished so that others can be promoted, in the minds of the selected; it is a place where emotion is given too much power, and is invoked for misplaced, often terrible purpose.

There are, thankfully, antitoxins for partisanism, for self-isolating groups, for cognitive clusters: real human contact, beyond memberships; real human dialog, beyond partisan sing-along; and real human fellowship, beyond partisan boundaries.

Tipping Point

We are at the tipping point of human history.

The population of the earth has more than doubled in our lifetimes, and will have tripled by the time we die.

We are a global community, deeply interdependent, for better or worse.

The forces of Authoritarianism, patriarchy, religion, and greed continue to struggle for supremacy.

The egalitarian struggles against the Authoritarian; the frightened struggle against the unafraid; the curious struggle against the cautious.

We have spent 10,000 years living in a false social bubble - and now there are too many of us to continue living in it.

We need to adapt. Or die.

Or do I overstate?

Empathy, yet again...

Some people have naturally high levels of empathy.

Some people have naturally low levels of empathy.

This is all to do with the amount of tissue they were born with in certain regions of their brains.

Our problem: people in each group feel that *their* natural empathy level is the correct one, and that others are off.

Our even-worse problem: people in each group form political parties together, elect others like them to high office, and create public policy that "seems right" to them, per their natural empathy levels.

AI and the Self

You have all heard me rail against the silly notions about AI that Hollywood has implanted in our national gestalt - that AI is a Frankenstein beast, destined to rage against us if unleashed; that it is the sword of Big Brother, poised to chop off our heads if we do not submit; that it will outgrow us, then squash our puny remnants.

Bullshit.

All of this trepidatious fantasy derives from misrepresentations of what AI is, seeded with misunderstanding of how both technology and consciousness really evolve. Artificial consciousness as we see it depicted in the movies - or even as conceived in the finest science fiction, or serious musings of subject matter experts - isn't something that can spontaneously emerge from the technology we use today; nor do we have sufficient knowledge or understanding of consciousness itself to intentionally design and implement such a thing.

What AI really is, and can be moving forward, is the extension and strengthening of those facets of thought and behavior that we *do* have sufficient knowledge and understanding of. It can be meaningfully applied in decision-making and the optimization of task execution, obviously, and that's where most efforts are focused; but the same technology that improves processes can be applied to improving behavior - that therein lies not our potential doom, but our potential salvation.

AI can learn when we stubbornly don't, at the personal level all the way out to the global; AI can spot the important things that we miss, and bring them to our attention; AI can note our disadvantageous behaviors and suggest improvements. It can study us as individuals more objectively and honestly than our closest friends and family; it can study our actions and our plans and recognize potential within us that even our own grandmothers never saw.

Artificial Intelligence isn't a digital monster tugging at the leash to attack and devour us; nor is it a digital weapon aimed between our eyes. It is a light that shines in places we didn't even know existed, to reveal and illuminate; it is an Honesty Machine, of value only when real and strong data are provided; it is no respecter of ideologies or dogma, but a courier of reality.

In the right hands, it is not simply a tool but a power source - a generator of human potential, a magnifying glass held above those noble inclinations that hide beneath the daily worries of us all. It can do more than empower us; it can ennoble us, unlocking our very best selves, as individuals and as a society.

Let's be the right hands.

The Dangers of a Blue Wave

If ever the stage was set for a Democratic sweep of midterm elections, it was set in November 2018.

And we needed it more than ever before - not because Democrats need to be dominant (they don't), or because progressive values are inherently superior (there's no such thing), or because the GOP needs to shrink and die (housecleaning will do).

We needed it because our democratic principles have been substantially dismantled, along with the machinery of government that has sustained the nation through its most prosperous era.

But that doesn't mean "victory" - it means stability. We need to stabilize a ship that is rocking to and fro precariously, lest we all wind up in the water.

For *either* side to dominate is a danger to what we as a nation are committed to being. We are a people of cooperation and compromise, by design; our Founders saw to it when they created our core architecture. We are a people intended to be invulnerable to tyranny, by the presence and power of the voices of the masses, the freedom of the press, the independence of our judiciary from partisan authority - a people who, by design, embrace multiple points of view.

Blue may have it in mind to put Red in its place once and for all - but in the words of Nietzsche, "When you fight the dragon, beware, lest ye become a dragon."

Blue has allowed itself to become enraged and incensed - and nothing productive ever comes of that. Blue has allowed itself to be lulled into a false sense of superiority - and nothing productive ever comes of that. Blue is imbued with the heady fragrance of its own righteousness - and nothing productive ever comes of that. In point of fact, these three characteristics are what gave rise to the current monstrosity of Red in the first place. It is deeply foolish to drink from that well.

But the biggest reason that Blue must continuously self-examine is far simpler: human beings *need* both blue and red, and all the blended hues between, in order to thrive; no one camp, no one ideology, no one social perspective or cognitive incline can deliver humankind into a healthy future - we are, by design, creatures who need our differences as much, if not more, than our similarities. The lesson of recent years is the inviability of one-party dominance.

Blue's best move is to be the adult; to eschew the temptation to grab the reins of power and beat down Red in the same style Red has made so popular, and return the nation to a more sensible, stable platform of inclusion, mutual acceptance, dialog and honorable opposition - to tune out the media hysteria and the banshees of both extremes, and to sit down at the table of cooperation with those who offered them no seat.

Red has demonstrated an inability to learn this lesson. If Blue fails as well, then we are trapped now and forevermore, fighting in a burning house...

Binkies

The conservatism I grew up in is unlikely to still exist when my children are my age. Neither will the liberalism of my youth. Both have morphed over the decades, for better or worse, and that morphing will continue.

Such 'ideologies' are largely reactions to prevailing conditions, rather than troves of moral and intellectual principles: individuals feel good about themselves when the tribe feels good, and the good feelings of tribes follow from features of the social landscape, not timeless truths. The latter are rationalizations, not principles.

That's what our children are inheriting - the residue of our social binkies, all slobbery and worn. They'd have been so much better off with a trove of authentic principle.

Huddles

A cognitive cluster is a natural huddle of people whose brains think in similar fashion – for instance, whose tendency toward risk aversion or social discomfort or desire for social hierarchy (or, conversely, hunger for consensus, indifference to risk, and discomfort with uniformity) cause them to feel more at ease when in each other's company, rather than among a random group.

These natural huddles occur because our brains 1) embrace simplicity, and cognitive clusters make life simpler; 2) our decision-making apparatus isn't really about reason; it's about the dopamine pleasure signal that dings in our brains when we are given emotional comfort by a conclusion, which may or may not actually derive from reason; and 3) we feel safe when everyone around us agrees, which in prehistoric times was a signal that the tribe was physically secure.

But our huddles, while understandable in our current social context, aren't healthy; they work in favor of the short-term satisfaction of the tribe, and against the long-term survival of our species. And they are not always cognitive.

Sometimes they're emotional.

We often cluster, for instance, around our innate levels of empathy.

Empathy is not a "decided" thing; it is not even, ultimately, an ideological or tribal thing. We each have a personal level of empathy, and we did not "choose" it, any more than we "choose" our eye color or aversion to broccoli. Empathy is a neurological process in the social area of the brain, a confluence of neural impulses from other parts of the brain, congregating in the insular cortex. Some of us are born with a great deal of tissue in the insula; some not so much. We don't decide this, and our parents' mating decisions do not take it into consideration.

Our experience in the world has some sway over how much of our social expression is empathetic, to be sure; within the range of impulses generated by our individual insulae, there can be (and invariably is) a low-to-high range of expression of empathy. But the bottom line is that some of us are born with a lot, some with a little, and some in-between.

Each of us as individuals considers our personal level of empathy to be "normal". Those who have only a modest amount look at those with more and think "bleeding heart!" Those with much look at those with less and think "heartless!"

And we naturally gravitate toward groups of people who are most like us in this regard. Our huddles, our clusters, are as emotional as they are cognitive.

We don't go out of our way to surround ourselves with people whose level of empathy is demonstrably more or less than our own; no high-empathy person sets out to be with those who have little; and no low-empathy group welcomes a "bleeding heart".

And this is a barrier to human cooperation, for as long as we have these huddles, these emotional clusters, we'll have political parties at odds, religions with their hackles up, and diminished unity in advancing the human race.

Two takeaways emerge from this line of thinking.

The first is that there is a way out - reduce the power of these clusters, by refusing to huddle in them. And the first step there is simple: we must each stop regarding our own level of empathy as "normal", and realize that there is no "normal", there are only points on a scale. "Normal" doesn't exist; we all just fall where we fall on that scale, and we all come by our personal level empathy honestly.

The second is this: we must stop demonizing one another for these differences. We must dispense with the scorn and derision heaped on those clustered individuals whose levels of empathy are not the same as ours.

This works in both directions, but I would lay it at the feet of those on the Left, whose outrage over the insensitivities of those on the Right drowns out much more pressing concerns - and is hypocritical besides, for the Left cannot rail about inequality and injustice and the idiocies of conservative bigotries if they themselves coddle this glaring emotional bigotry.

For it is just as wrong to serve up disdain for a person whose empathy is less than our own than for a person of color or differing sexual orientation. Empathy, like sexuality and gender and skin color and eye color and metabolism and a spectrum of cognitive traits, is ultimately genetic. The Left doesn't get to be morally superior for traits inherited from one's genes.

This line of reasoning is bumpy terrain, because it pushes against our prejudices and our emotional wants - we *want* to believe that our normal is *the* normal; we *want* to believe we are morally superior. We naturally resist any assertion that we are not.

But I would argue that those are exactly the impulses that reduce the moral progress we are seeking. They are odds with our quest to reduce inequality and bigotry. They push down our more noble impulses.

Our huddles, our ignoble impulses, our moral superiority - all of them hurt us, none of them help us. And the solution to each is the same - a matter of each of us, as individuals, letting go.

Ideology

Ideological framings of human nature will always, always fail us; they will always suppress our most honest evaluation and appreciation of one another - for ideologies are subjective, never completely honest, and selectively appreciative, often in craven ways. By their nature, they suppress the cooperation that enables humankind to move forward.

We are not naturally ideological; we are natural cooperators, the greatest nature has ever produced. We stumble in that cooperation in our current state, which has lasted several thousand years now, for a number of reasons - but the greatest is exactly that: the emotional gratifications of clinging to ideology.

Energy Coupons

We need a new economic model. The old ones are no longer working (assuming they ever did).

We can view money at its most basic level as a stand-in for something else: food, water, clothing, shelter, etc. this definition stretches across recorded history.

Put another way, money is an energy coupon.

Now - in more modern times - money is certification of production. The creation of value, encoded.

Extending the frame, a new economics might do well to enshrine the laws of thermodynamics...

Artificial Intelligence and the US Worker

Robots are breeding like rabbits. AI-driven workflow is infiltrating business at all levels, distributed via the Smart Cloud (and this is not hyperbole, folks; the Smart Cloud is Uncle Scott's domain, and trust me, it really has arrived).

AI can do *all* of the work of 25% of the US office workforce; it can do 50% or more of the work of more than half of the rest. And those numbers will rise steadily from here on out. They should terrify us.

But the greatest casualty of AI will *not* be the US worker; it will be the economic ideologies that have led us to this inescapable corner, the Adam Smith Died for Your Sins thinking of those who have built their entire perception of human nature around the imaginary imbisible hand.

I have said elsewhere that the vanities of US sports folded like an accordion at the first punch of sabermetrics; how long can our craven political ideologies hold out, when the lowliest of our international neighbors are running rings around us?

On the Nature of a Book

A few moments ago, I found myself trying to read from a book with one hand and type with the other. This posture is non-optimal for either activity.

Annoyed, I acquiesced to the book's demands. And I suddenly felt a wave of humility and contrition sweep over me. The book did not grin in triumph, it did not gloat or preen; instead, it nestled gratefully into my hands, smiled up at me and said, 'Thank you!'

Way back in 1984, I wrote a column for a newspaper that quoted sociologist Tony Campolo, who was arguing vociferously against the advent of technology in storytelling. His ire was leveled in particular against *Star Wars*, which was still fresh, and within which the rapidity of sensory assault had (at that time) set a new world record, with its relentless blasts of sounds and images and musical bombast. Campolo's argument: whatever happened to books? Whatever happened to the simplicity of opening a book and turning on the mind?

Well, I don't need to be sold; I possess almost as many books as I have body hairs - but the brief, non-textual exchange I had with this particular book in this particular moment offered up a new thought.

A book, by design, demands all of me.

I need both hands to hold it. Oh, I can hold a book in one hand, size and weight allowing, but I still need my other hand to turn the page. I need both station and calm to engage with it, for the required posture demands full attention; I need tranquility to fully receive it, for it makes uncompromising calls on my eyes, mind, and memory.

Of course, we live in a world that isn't all books and summer blockbusters - in between we find all manner of reading material, enmeshed in varying tangles of technology. I read from screens all day long, and they do not make the intimate demands of the book; I can nudge them along with a tap on a screen or a tease of a mouse. My attention can be - indeed, most often *must* be - fragmented at best, for any screen I admit will be an arena of playground antics, competing for my eyes.

Then there are the non-digital remnants of my youth - newspapers and magazines, book-like in structure but more akin to digital screens in substance. Here, too, there is much noise, all too little intimacy, and no embrace is called for.

It's the embrace, I think, that is finally the point.

A book calls out to the reader's senses. The pages of a book greet the reader's fingertips like nothing else that fingers ever touch, warm and even and slightly grainy. It has a certain smell that only books – especially new ones! - have. We've all been in libraries; is there any other building that smells like one?

And that unique scent changes over time; I remember the attic of my mother's father's home, where many bookcases stuffed with ancient paperbacks lived, and how different it smelled than any other room. That scent always reminds me of him, a kind and quiet man of much unspoken thought and private wisdom, and how he would bring me a book with every visit, or have a new one waiting when our family would visit him, and how that ritual made me who I am today.

All of these features of a book coalesce into a demand for my consummate attention, and that attention includes not just my mind but my full touch and sensory engagement. The book will settle for nothing less than a tactile relationship - like the child who extends her arms, wishing to be picked up, or the lover who wants to be held. When I enter into congress with a book, our exchange admits no other party; interruption is unwelcome, and even music in the background must be unobtrusive. It is our private occasion, and no one else's.

I didn't think it was possible for me to love books more; today, once again, I learned a little something.

Parental

There's a moment most of us experience in life that changes us more than any other - that instant when we become a parent, when we see our newborn child for the first time. In that instant, a vast assortment of new emotions, priorities, and impulses suddenly unpack themselves in our hearts and brains, and we become someone new.

Amid this unpacking is an entirely new definition of the word "responsibility". We realize that this new life is in our hands, and that realization restructures everything about our own. We must now take better care of ourselves; we must be wiser in our allocation of time; we must keep a closer eye on money, and so on. These things aren't even a question; they are just a sudden new reality that is accepted unconditionally.

This same dynamic exists in another domain, though we have been conditioned to think around it, rather than address it: our role in governing ourselves.

We in the US do not bow to a monarch or dictator; we are, by design, a self-governing people. That is, we set our own destiny, entitled to do so by no means other than our citizenship. We ponder our identity, we scrutinize our national history and destiny, we deliberate with others and engage in public discourse over the decisions that affect our course - and we choose, with the greatest care, the administrators who will implement those decisions.

This is the gift we received from our Founding Fathers - men without title, citizens who formed a nation out of nothing but ideas and determination. They were men of vision and talent, to be sure, but they were men - just a bunch of guys who realized things needed to change, that they could be made better, and that it wouldn't happen if they didn't make it happen.

Now here's the disconnect: we call them 'Founding Fathers,' and they were - parents to a nation, rising to that huge responsibility that settles upon the procreator in the moment of a new birth. They handled it well, comporting themselves as any new parent, investing in the new life they'd brought into the world, resolved in their commitment and dedication and their very best efforts.

And somewhere along the way, in calling them 'Fathers', we have created the idea that we are, conversely, 'children'.

We are not.

We are not the children of Jefferson, Madison, Franklin, Adams, Hamilton, and the others who created this wonderful shared life we look after - we are their successors.

We are parents, charged with caring for and nourishing and protecting a life. The United States is not our 'parent' - it is our child, still growing, still learning, still struggling to mature. And our responsibility to this sacred charge is as parental as our call to provide for our own literal young - a responsibility to self-improve, to embrace commitment, diligence, self-awareness, and all the other virtues that such responsibility requires of us.

Chief among these are fidelity to knowledge and the truth.

Among the inborn impulses that unpack within us at the advent of parenthood is the desire to learn - from peers, experts, books, any reasonable source - how to do this child-rearing thing well. Even if we grew up well-parented ourselves, even if we were raised in part by an older sibling or aunt/uncle/grandparent, we still strive to learn all we can about our new role. We become more observant; we ask more questions of others; we pay more attention to the world.

And, finally, we let go of a lot of bullshit. We say goodbye to those things in our lives that might hinder us, including the lies we have self-indulgently told ourselves about what's good and bad for us - and, looking forward, what's good and bad for our new child.

That's harder to do when the child being nurtured is a nation, because our parental charge is shared with more than just a single co-parent - but just as Mom and Dad must often work through differences in viewpoint about what's best for baby, discussing and compiling new information and consulting those with more experience, we have it within our grasp to commit to what's real and what's not and what's healthy and not and what's true and not.

Would we compromise that commitment to truth and reality by nodding along with the tribe if our child's well-being was at stake? Of course not. Why, then, are we so casual with reality and truth and our commitment to seeking them out and adhering to them when the health of our nation is in the balance?

As parents, we commit to improve ourselves, in order to enrich our children. As self-governing citizens, we are essentially parents. Our elected leaders are not the parents; they are those we hire for a time to help look after the child - this growing, restless, occasionally tantrum-throwing, immature entity we call the United States.

Like all children, it requires from each of us all those virtues set forth above - and, of course, it begs our love, even when it isn't particularly lovable.

And love requires our very best, even as it makes us better.

Cooperation's Bad Name

Cooperation has gotten a bad name. "Consensus-building" has ceased to be a virtue.

This is wrong. This is backward. We are natural cooperators, and we have survived 300,000 years through consensus behaviors. We have created a fake world wherein we have jacked up "competition" and "opposition" beyond all reason, to the point where we can't get anything done at all.

"Competition" and "opposition" are how lone predators survive in the wild.

They're how the lion and the cheetah and the saber tooth made meals of us.

One man alone against a saber tooth is cat food; eight men with spears against a saber tooth eat well that night.

Cooperation and consensus-building are our legacy, our strength, our future. Don't let the predators tell you any different.

AI, Jesus, and Purity of Thought

I'm the last person you'll ever hear using the computer-brain metaphor - *"Your brain is like a computer, and your thoughts are like software!"* Having professional oars in the waters of both artificial intelligence and neuropsychology, I'm very clear that brains and computers are not only not the same thing but complements by design: the brain does well what computers cannot, and computers do well what brain cannot.

And yet the lines are blurring. This very day, I'm working on an artificial intelligence project - 'machine learning' - where a model of a snippet of reality is built up in a computer, and the model is designed to anticipate human behavior. The system 1) learns, as people do (through experience, not explicit programming), 2) about the thoughts of people.

So today I'm going to break my own rule and indulge the metaphor. Two hundred millennia before Turing conceived of the computer, human beings were already doing what I describe above – modeling snippets of reality, building a limited 'copy' of the real world in memory and referring to it at will – and running 'simulations,' which we think of as imagination. The human brain is flush with cerebral tissue, a boon of evolution that allows us this inner white board of the world. We can build up, in our individual minds, personal models of the world that allow us to anticipate and understand it, as my project mentioned above will hopefully do, and understand, in turn, each other and ourselves.

My first point: we spend as much or more time living in our models as we do in reality.

Make a project of it: for the next few days, make a note in your phone or tablet every time you find yourself reviewing a recent conversation, or rehearsing an upcoming one, or pondering the behaviors of Trump voters, or judging those in power, or feeling triggered by an episode of *Friends*, or wandering in your mind back to your childhood during a dull sermon, or earworming a song from the Seventies. Compare that to the amount of time you spend in actual conversation or real-time information-gathering. I'll bet the ratio you come up with is 20:1, at a minimum.

We spend a lot of time in our inner models! We review, we rehearse, we rewrite, we revise, we re-examine. Constantly. It's how we're designed.

And this is how AI works: machine learning is exactly the same process – running through events over and over and over, culling little clues about reality from models that try to replicate it, capturing useful insights about how it truly works and what we can reasonably expect.

My second point: Jesus had this figured out long, long ago.

Oftentimes, our inner and outer worlds don't match. It is the norm, not the exception, that the model of the world in our heads differs from what's real – and that we actively feed those gaps.

Some may imagine motivations in others that don't exist.

Some invent justifications for their own behavior when they know them to be contrived.

Some fantasize they are with someone other than their partner when they're with their partner.

Some conjure scenes of revenge against those who have done them harm.

Some envision succeeding and accomplishing in place of others. Some visualize getting even with an ex.

Some treat things that are perfectly safe as dangerous; some imagine dangerous things to be safe.

The list is endless. Our inner model of the world becomes a theater of indulgence, where our imagined reality becomes more satisfying than our actual reality.

But surely this isn't harmful in itself? Isn't the what-if functionality of our inner world the foundation of creativity, invention, and inspiration?

It can be all those things, and often is. But that requires discipline and self-awareness, and both are hard to come by.

It's important to note that when we describe our inner-world activities as 'satisfying,' we mean that literally – it is satisfactory in the same way the real world is satisfactory. It gives us the same dopamine fix, the same feelings of 'rightness' - all the emotional cues offered up by the real world... but under our selective influence.

That's where we get into trouble. We can enjoy life in our inner-world model, where our illusions might provide outcomes and validations the real world may withhold, more than our actual lives.

She Is Anyway

I can understand someone selling poppies from a tray in the middle of the roundabout - nice, central location, good visibility (though you'd have to cut through busy traffic from any point, which is not optimal) - but why *behind* the shelter? It's *pouring rain!* Better to be *in* the shelter, maybe?

Won't the pretty nurse get soaking wet? Won't the tray fill up with water? And how does any of this feel like "being in a play?"

Very strange...

The Opinion and the Person

We tend to focus on the opinion of the person offering it, rather than the person; we tend to judge the person by the opinion, rather than the other way around.

This is not only a wasted opportunity to expand our understanding of the person (and, by extension, ourselves, and people in general), it serves up a far less accurate assessment of both the opinion and the person; we tend to rate the opinion in comparison to our own, and then rate the person in comparison to ourselves - which leads us to assign more value people whose opinions are closer to our own, and less value to those who are farther afield.

This isn't honest, helpful, or even healthy.

If we were to make the subtle but important shift to paying attention to the person, over and above their opinion, we would acquire a better understanding of both - and more realistically see ourselves in the spectrum of humanity.

Finally, focusing on the opinion rather than its author immediately locks us into subconsciously scanning for difference - whereas focusing on the person moves us toward subconsciously scanning for similarity. That in itself is a game-changer: when we are attentive to those things which unite us, rather than those things which divide us, we all become stronger.

The Strange Loops That Are Me

In my recent book *The Children of Babel*, I mention Douglas Hofstadter's 'strange loops' - self-referential recursions that pop up in our art, mathematics, logic and music, echoing structures of thought inside our minds. This is a powerful, elegant, and useful way of understanding consciousness, and I tried to celebrate it in the book.

Hofstadter took the idea to a new level in his 2007 book, *I Am a Strange Loop*, when he added a new piece to his own theory of consciousness. He has long mourned his wife Carol, who died suddenly on vacation in Italy, leaving him inconsolable. The new piece is this: he began to identify, within his own thinking and perception, bits and pieces of thought that he realized he had inherited from Carol, during their marriage - and realized that the strange loops that give him his sense of self - his "I" - are more than a little Carol.

What a beautiful, powerful idea! My own contribution is the notion that this feature of consciousness may be a defining component - that it is the strange loops of others like ourselves, taken into our own, that enable consciousness as we experience it.

In support of this idea, we may look to feral children, who - absent human contact through their formative years - never acquire language and who remain animal-like in their behaviors. We might also study how isolated babies, raised in European orphanages, grow up with serious cognitive and social deficits - or how isolation later in life hastens cognitive deterioration.

But it's more interesting still to examine our own strange loops in the context of our loved ones. Per Hofstadter, this taking-on of the strange loops of others - the bits and pieces of how they enter and experience the world - occurs between intimates. And all of us experience intimacy, in varying degrees, from birth till death: our parents, our children, our spouses, our close friends - giving us ample opportunity to intermingle our strange loops.

And 'intimate' doesn't always mean 'positive,' as we infer in Hofstadter's references to his marriage; we can be intimately entangled with people who do us harm: an unloving parent, a domineering partner, a passive-aggressive friend - and find ourselves taking on, unconsciously, patterns of thought and reference that diminish, rather than augment, our own experience of self, others, and the world.

We can realize that our intimacy in some relationships is finite, and that we have reached an ending - and can choose to locate those strange loops that passed between us, and embrace them as treasures to be cherished long after our parting. What can be done?

To begin with, we can begin a project of introspection - to self-examine, in reflection, those bits and pieces of our conscious thoughts and perceptions that distinctly match what we observe in those we love or once loved, and enhance our awareness of this contribution to our own lives. We can see if it's possible to pick and choose, through heightened awareness, what to take on from those with whom we are currently intimate, or whatever this process is completely passive.

We can wonder, and perhaps explore, whether there's a 'threshold' of intimacy that triggers the embedding of another's strange loops. And do we each have our own threshold, or is it a general human thing?

Finally, we can wonder - just how much 'me' is inherited from others? What parts of me are authentically me, only me, and not borrowed? Any at all? Hofstadter offers no answers to any of these questions - he gives us only a starting point. But what a wonderful undertaking, for any among who choose to take it further?

Men and Women

One of the loudest protests leveled at the Far Right is its explicit dedication to generating, and forcing everyone else to live in, an alternate reality.

For sure Trump's reality is contrived - and, for sure, we've been subjected to a steady GOP retreat from reality for the past 25 years.

But *all* of us, to some degree, live in an alternate reality, because cognitive clusters (large social groups made up of people who have the same cognitive patterns and biases) generate alternate realities by their very nature.

Here's a new one: Men and Women.

I have, for a long while now, been confronted with the timeless parade of gender generalizations that we so easily fall prey to - when women speak of "men" as if all men behave the same way or have the same biases and prejudices, and men speaking of "women" the same way.

Easy to fall prey to, but fallacious. By the same cognitive features that generate the diversity we see in our social frameworks, "men" and "women" are not two categories, but many.

There is, in fact, virtually *no* statement any of us can utter, in terms of declaring properties of gender, that turns out to be true: "All men..." just about has to end with "...have penises!" in order be a defensible statement.

And the same is true (and even more so, when we are in the domain of social and cognitive biases) with statements beginning with "All women..."

As is so often the case, we need to be screening our pronouncements about others not only for bias but for assumptions, each and every time we decide to utter one. It's not just that we run the risk of saying something that isn't true, and therefore isn't useful; it's that what we say perpetuates a falsehood that puts yet another tear in the fabric of actual reality.

Gaps

Let's revisit our Paleo past once again.

This human tribe, here along the banks of what will one day be the Ruvumaa River – let's follow them a while.

There are 107 of them, ranging in age from newborn to 32. They are spread out at the moment in four separate groups, across a couple of square miles, with a hunting party out and another preparing to leave. The 32-year-old, that woman over there by the fire, nursing her sister's three-year-old, has survived more than half a dozen cat attacks: she limps a little; she won't survive the next one.

The young man behind her, the one cutting jerky, is one of her three husbands. She has fewer than her sisters, but that's not because she's older; it's because she's choosier. She's as fit as they are, and wiser, and is in a three-way tie for having the most surviving offspring in the group.

She was born into a neighboring tribe to the north, and migrated into this one 21 years ago. She and a sister were part of a hunting party that met a hunting party from this tribe, and they liked what they smelled.

See those nine over there, packing rations and checking weapons? They're going on a long hunt. They'll be gone between three and five days. They're headed southwest; a scout (our 32-year-old's oldest son) found herdsign, odd for this time of year. Five men, four women – all but two are teenagers.

The morning passes, and the hunting party is on its way. Each of the four camps sends out gathering teams to score veggies for the evening meal. Each team has a couple of armed guards, and eyes scanning for cats. Children are necessarily in each group; they are constantly learning, and have been taught duck-and-cover. And each child is surrounded by parents, for all parents in this tribe are parents to all children. Every child is of equal value to every adult.

By next month, one of these gathering adults and one of the children will be taken by cats, and the tribe's population will drop to

105; but only briefly, as a baby will be born immediately after, and three more in summer, two of which will survive to adulthood. At any given moment, between six and 10 of the tribe's females are pregnant.

Though the guards are vigilant, there has been no cat seen near this part of the river for days. The youngers know to be quiet while gathering, but there is still some soft play, grins and a bit of fun. Mothers and fathers praise successful finds. They return to their various camps well-stocked.

The evening fires are large and bright, the meat is warm, the water cool, and the skies above are filled with smiling gods. There is laughter and play; small children are cuddled and nursed, larger children are experimenting with cuddling.

Wood has been gathered for every fire; tenders have been selected. There will soon be sleep; but first the 32-year-old begins to sing, softly chanting a sad, sweet melody, and others join in. The youngest drift off, safe in the arms of whichever parent is closest; females call for their partners, and loving begins; sentries turn their attention to the dark, scanning for tiny pairs of green eyes.

All is well along this stretch of the Ruvuma River.

I described this scene to make a point.

These people were real. They lived together, loved together, died together, and did so in the manner described above (though only a smattering of detail is presented here). They were families – superfamilies, much larger than ours and far more intimate – in one another's presence, 24/7. They were under predation their entire lives. We know with confidence that few ever made it to age 40, not because they weren't healthy and genetically fit, but because they were food for large cats.

They did not have writing, but they had language – and art, and song, and stories. Their lives were rich and full and deeply intertwined. There was no loneliness and isolation in this way of living; there was community and intimacy and empathy and a fullness of experience that we can scarcely conceive of.

And the point is this: these people knew one another fully. They were the natural expression of the homo sapien brain, which contains areas that evolved specifically to optimize their collective survival. Put another way, there is a human 'social brain' nested within the overall brain, and the family described above represents that brain's ideal use.

A human being can know and understand and love about 150 others. That's called Dunbar's Number, and it's a measure of the amount of tissue in the homo sapien brain set aside for processing information about living among others of our kind. And when we say "know and understand and love," we mean knowing and understanding and loving as we did 100,000 years ago.

Those relationships were far more complete than ours, far closer, far more intimate; there was daily input, daily encounter, constant update – all relationships remained current, except during those brief periods when some family members were away on a hunt.

There were no gaps in those relationships. All stood side-by-side; partners were always there; children were always loved. No gaps.

One hundred thousand years later, gaps are everywhere.

Today, we no longer live and love and die together. We are raised in virtual isolation, with only a handful in close proximity; parents are distracted, children often left to figure it out; mates are disenchanted, and deceit is common; trust is rare, suspicion constant. Even in safe, strong communities, intimacy is discouraged, kept at the most casual level.

Rather than living among intimates, joining in song each night, we each consider each ourselves lucky if we have as many as two or three truly intimate friends – and mates who love one another with life-or-death commitment are discouragingly rare. Children no longer grow up enshrouded in the warm certainty of acceptance; they grow up desperately hoping for it.

There are many gaps in these relationships.

There are many degrees of social connection today, rather than a few; some have only existed briefly - "casual", "acquaintance" - and some horrific new ones, inconceivable in the past for the risk to the tribe they would impart: "antagonist", "assailant", "tormenter".

And however close to or far away from the people around us we find ourselves, we now accept that there will be gaps in our knowledge or understanding of them. In our ancient past, those gaps could be fatal: on a hunt, or in the brush, searching for food, it was a survival imperative to be fully aware of those nearby, and mindful of their likely behavior.

Today, there are gaps between each of us and our colleagues; our friends, close and distant; between parents and children; between mates. Our society is Swiss-cheesed with these gaps.

And our social brain doesn't like gaps; it wants continuous understanding of those it thinks our lives depend upon. So we fill in the gaps in our knowledge and understanding of everyone, from our closest intimate to our most casual acquaintance to our worst enemies.

We fill those gaps with fantasy; with gossip; with supposition; with transference; with anxiety; with wish fulfillment; with social media memes. We fill those gaps with everything but reality, because we've built a world that no longer permits us the luxury of truly intimate community, truly contiguous experience.

Perhaps the greatest casualty of gaps is this...

Observing 32, watching her living alongside her tribe and loving each member, we cannot miss the fact that these are creatures who not only experience far deeper, far more pervasive empathy than we do today – their very lives depend upon it. They literally could not survive without empathy as the principle driver of their community and personal bonds.

In our world of gaps, we have excised empathy. We dismiss human beings by the hundreds of millions, erasing their humanity as an unnecessary abstraction, just to make room for the people closest by, to lighten our emotional load. Empathy, that which asks the most of us, goes out the window.

We can't fill in the gaps in our relationships with knowledge and experience – we don't have enough sources for all the knowledge nor time for the missing experience. But if each of us took the time to consider each of our relationships, from the closest to the most distant, identifying the gaps in each – and then committed to simply filling those gaps with empathy, rather than gossip or assumption or fantasy – what kind of world would result?

Our brains can't produce enough to fill every single gap – but imagine what would happen if we filled every one we could?

Less Real

"Would you call yourself an atheist?" my Christian friend from my church years asked.

"I would never use that word," I answered carefully, "but I probably meet your definition of it."

"Why wouldn't use it, then?" he asked. "What's the difference?"

"It's a nonsensical word," I replied. "It's ultimately a meaningless term, and so I can't see applying it to myself." (I have issues with how we constrain our experience of others when we categorize them in general, but that was too deep a dive for the conversation)

"An atheist," he said simply, "is someone who doesn't believe in God."

"Exactly," I answered, "and if we define it all the way, then you and I are not going to be able to meaningfully agree on the definition of either 'believe' or 'God' - because those definitions change to suit context. And so there's no real point in living inside that label. It doesn't mean anything real, and living inside it just makes me less real..."

If I define myself in meaningless terms, I'm living a meaningless life.

Noise

I campaign tirelessly for those on *any* side of our modern predicament to check their contempt and disdain at the door, and take the risk of truly understanding *why* those who behave and vote and post inexplicably do so. Any other course obscures real answers and creates noise for those of us who pursue them.

And that noise is present among my friends, too, every day, to my disappointment.

I am by no means innocent. Years ago, I was as disdainful and as contemptuous. Knowledge, new information about what human beings really are, how we came to be and what we are capable of, turned me around.

Immerse Yourself

Immerse yourself in activities that threaten to change your thinking.

Take a class you would normally avoid. Volunteer for a service that makes you uncomfortable. Join a group where you will have to defend yourself and your views.

Such choices make you a stronger individual - and a worthier contributor to the world around you.

AI's Bad Rap

Artificial Intelligence has gotten a bad rap, thanks to Stanley Kubrick and James Cameron and other cinematic gadflies: it is presented as the culmination of the Frankenstein myth, a distillation of our fears of the evil that lurks in the hearts of men, set in silicon. I have always taken this to be sensationalist bullshit - but when we look at the ominous punditry surrounding the intrusion of AI into our healthcare and our banking and our automobiles, it's easy to see that the effects of HAL and SkyNet linger on.

Artificial Intelligence is, in the end, something less than the creation of imitation people and something more than glorified UI. It is a means to an end, and my argument is that it is going to become the most important means to the most important end: the management of that which is best of human thought and feeling, dedicated to the enrichment of all human experience.

Artificial Intelligence can do for humankind what amplifiers did for guitars: it can take the power of a simple campfire song and send it out into the night sky to inspire not just the handful around the fire, but all the cheering masses, swaying as one to a thrilling, unifying anthem; it can restore the balance between these minds and those minds, shattered now by the atrophy of thoughts-of-least-resistance, sharpening our ideas and strengthening our feelings and reminding us who we really are, beyond the safety of our Facebook groups and favorite TV channels. It can become the mirror we need and deserve, so much more honest and effective than the partisan yowl of Twitter. It can be the stone knife that separates meat from bone in our mental feeding, the bearskin that warms us as clouds of uncertainty gather above.

It can be the nurturing of our very best selves, the light that shatters the shadow of exploitation, and the renewed reach of the hand of cooperation.

Hot Nerd Talk

So what are you wearing right now?

An Apple watch

Tell me EVERYTHING you're wearing right now!

An Apple watch

See, now I won't be able to work

Focus, perv boy

Does our planned rendezvous remain propitious?

You mean are we still going out this weekend?
It depends. What do you have in mind?

Your most indulgent culinary preferences, followed by stimulating cultural
exhibitions, followed by private repose in either of our domiciles

Ah

Private repose, you say

Salubrious interpersonal congress, frivolous persiflage, moderate ingestion
of vintage ethanol, accompanied by the finest recordings of the most
notable post-Enlightenment troubadours

Caruso? Ghiaurov?

I was thinking Barry White

followed by a precoital osculation interregnum

Osculation?

Or suaviation, if you like
Whatever your term of preference, it is the transfer of testosterone from my
bloodstream to yours, through absorption by your oral mucosa, followed by
immediate conversion to estradiol by aromatase
This will lead to a comfortable state of mutual dishabille

I'm swooning

Next will come manual invigoration of the epidermis, eliciting the release of
copious quantities of oxytocin

swoon swoon

and prolactin

:p

extending gradually to include piquant oral exploration
of your areolae, perineum, and introitus - all of which will increase
receptivity to penetration

You make it sound so very hot

I know, right?

Well don't stop now, you're on a roll

We will then proceed to DNA transfer

:p

This activity will culminate with fecund intimate congress, initiated with the
invigoration of the crura through the anterior mucosa wall

Invigoration...

Invigoration, followed by invagination, followed by insemination

'Invagination' isn't a word

Mr. Webster begs to differ

Sounds somewhat invasive

It is not without its rewards
Properly executed and sufficiently sustained, it will provide you with
repeated spasmic contractions of your pubococcygeus muscle

:p

By the way, you haven't asked me what I'm wearing

Pray tell

My Batman onesie

See, now I won't be able to work

The Selfish Group

Richard Dawkins' famous, fascinating book *The Selfish Gene* did much to focus the understanding of how human behavior evolved on the individual - and this was a bomb blast among many in the struggle between models of selection being argued in the 1960s-70s.

But group selection has prevailed over the past couple of decades, despite the objections of Dawkins, Robert Sapolsky and others. E.O. Wilson led the charge in the opposite direction (see *Sociobiology*), and has steadily withstood challenge after challenge over the decades.

Then there's William Hamilton, who made the case mathematically for kin selection (Marshall Sahlins had made a similar case, anthropologically), which sits somewhere in between. The argument is that an individual will serve his/her genes by sacrificing self for kin - since kin carry the same genes. So altruistic action can be seen as genetically linked. This view gained ground quickly.

Pushing the argument further in Wilson's direction was the contribution of George Price to Hamilton's work. He demonstrated, mathematically, that altruistic behaviors themselves serve the same purpose as kin selection, implying that genetic transmission is *not* the only path for conveying survival advantage: when I, an altruist, gather together with other altruists, they need not all share genes with me in order for the genetic advantage of altruism to propagate. A mechanism *other than* genes now exists for the perpetuation of a survival advantage - a purely social mechanism. (And the same, of course, applies to any shared group behaviors with survival advantage, not just altruism.)

This is huge, and Price's work - not fully understood, initially - now stands as a major pillar in the work done in evolutionary biology since the 1970s. But its implications are ominous, as Price himself lamented, and they impinge on the notions about Cognitive Clustering – unhealthy concentrations of the like-minded – discussed elsewhere in this book.

Cognitive Clustering is basically a label for this social transmission method that Price has identified.

When individuals gather together into social groups for the purpose of reinforcing behaviors that convey advantage to them personally, they enhance their survival prospects for themselves and their group - but they diminish the prospects for other groups. Put another way, if Price's theory of social transmission of survival advantage is correct, then we are *naturally compelled* to Cognitive Clustering - it's not just a convenient dopamine *ding*.

This is a prospect that casts a dark shadow over our prospects as a species. What are we to do?

Living in the Future

In 30 years, I've flown 150 times or so, and I always look forward to seeing the lights of civilization below me at night or in early morning. I always find myself reflecting on how new this experience truly is, and how lucky I am to have been born when I was...

- When my grandparents were born, airplanes had not yet been invented;

- When their parents were born, electric lights had not yet been invented;

- When their parents were born, industry as we know it was in its first generation;

- When their parents were born, we were not yet running civilization on fossil fuel power.

And closer to our own lives...

- When my parents were born, human beings had yet to surpass the speed of sound;

- When I was born, we were just beginning to leave the earth;

- When I finished grade school, the first integrated circuit had just been developed;

- When I entered high school, computers the size of shoeboxes had been achieved;

- When I was in college, the first reusable space vehicles began flying;

- When I started my career, shoebox-sized computers became commercial and widely distributed;

- When my children were in grade school, all the computers in the world got connected to each other;

- When I crossed into middle age, all those devices became wireless;

- When my kids became adults, our telephones and computers and entertainment all merged into one.

And today, I can interact with whomever I please, anywhere in the world, on demand, in real time, for free.

Richard Deming's "The Shape of Things That Came" is a little-known but insightful sci-fi story about a time traveler in 1900 who goes ahead 50 years, sees the wonder of fast cars and air travel and an increasingly technological society, returns to 1900 and writes about it - only to be rejected.

"It's not that the wonders you write about are not credible," says the rejecting editor, "What's not believable is that people living in 1950, some of whom are living today, could possibly *take such a world for granted..."*

More Empathy

Our emotional identification with other human beings - is the result of activity in a very specific part of the brain. Human beings vary considerably in the empathy that they experience: some have none at all (we call such a person a sociopath), some have an overwhelming excess (we call such a person a 'bleeding heart').

When one focuses on this factor of human social processing in evaluating political attitudes, it becomes easy to consider the activities of leaders and policymakers in terms of the relative level of empathy at work in the acting individual. Indeed, our personal perceptions of human nature are a direct result of our individual capacity for empathy.

Racism, nationalism, globalism, misogyny, inclusiveness, exclusiveness, social classes and castes, inequality, democracy, autocracy --- all of these sociopolitical phenomena boil down to variability in empathy.

It may be time to start using empathy as an overt measure of fitness to lead - and to recognize that when sameness-in-empathy causes groups to form, any such group will become both predictable and naturally suspect, with regard to its prescriptions for all...

The Man Without a Party

I have this friend. I've known him a long while, and we've had many satisfying discussions, both with each other and in groups with others. He comes from the world I once belonged to – white middle class, conservative, church-going. We differ here and there on this or that social or economic issue, but despite our political divide, we enjoy our frequent exchanges.

I hasten to point out that my white middle class conservative church-going friend is not the sort of person who conforms to that description today: he is no extremist, no right-wing hate-monger, no echo chamber chorus boy; he is, rather, a thoughtful, moderately inclined man of strong character and ethical resolve. That makes it my pleasure to seek him out for discourse on important matters - I invariably benefit from his input.

My friend has a problem. It is not an uncommon problem. A longtime Republican, he stares out at the political landscape today and no longer sees the welcoming edifice he used to call home. He describes this change, as so many moderate, reasonable Republicans do, by saying, "I didn't leave my party; my party left me." The phrase originated with Ronald Reagan, describing his transition from Democrat to Republican, decades ago; but we hear it increasingly on the other side of the fence today, as the GOP has relentlessly purged itself of moderates and 'compromisers' in its quest for one-party dominance and ideological 'purity'.

We can view this extremist obsession with unvarying like-mindedness as the most blatant expression of a phenomenon that defines the social toxicity of the modern era: cognitive clustering, the social affiliation of a great many people in servitude to some sort of politically or ideologically motivated agenda, one that requires their absolute unquestioning loyalty. The cognitive effect of such clusters is a deliberate cessation of critical thinking, a members-only agreement that the group's thoughts and positions must be the thoughts and positions of every individual, with banishment from the group as consequence for any heretical expression that might contradict the collective rhetoric. The phenomenon is neither recent nor exclusively political; the patriarchal religions – Christianity and

Islam in particular – have practiced this clustering for centuries, often elevating the penalty for violation to gruesome death.

Like so many, my friend did not explicitly choose to leave his party - his party simply migrated far beyond the principles he personally embraces, and made abundantly clear that the services of those like him, who did not approve, were no longer needed or wanted. Thus my friend is now 'politically homeless' - another increasingly common label.

The same has happened in the world of religion in the US, where so many of my friends who were part of the Evangelical Christian church have found the church leaving them behind in its reckless quest to shovel coal into the engine of the rising GOP beast. They didn't want to leave; they are still as spiritual as ever, and as committed to their principles as ever – but their failure to endorse their church's politics and social agenda has left them unwanted and viewed with suspicion.

My friends from both groups, who now live in increasing isolation, suddenly find themselves in many ways lonely and disheartened.

To my friend – and to all in similar straits – I would offer the following thoughts:

A cognitive cluster – be it a religion, a political party, a social class, an ideological camp - is no place for a person of conscience, for the conscience is the province of the individual, the most personal and intimate terrain of conviction and principle and ethical commitment; it may not be farmed out to any group, and is imperiled when treated so;

A cognitive cluster is no place for a person of independent thought, for critical thought requires the whetstone of debate, opposing views, and challenges both intellectual and emotional, in broad measure;

A cognitive cluster is no place for a person of empathy and compassion, for clusters are anti-diversity by their very nature – and the honing of empathy and compassion requires diversity, the knowing and loving of persons of all kinds, to have any real meaning;

A cognitive cluster is no place for a person of honesty and integrity, for clusters require the sacrifice of both in the service of emotional fictions designed to soothe the dissonance of their members.

In short, cognitive clusters are unhealthy places – and the loneliness that sweeps over those who find themselves free of them may be seen as an inevitable but necessary convalescence.

And, of course, not all social groups are cognitive clusters; one need not belong to a church, a political party or an ideological camp to have a true home. When one steps out of a tent and into an encampment, nothing is lost but the previous isolation; all of the opportunity and richness and sunlight and fresh air of the human experience are retained, each in greater measure.

Put another way, my friend is not homeless at all; in standing for his principles, in being willing to be left behind, rather than become something he would abhor, he has simply stepped beyond the lesser tribe, and affirmed his well-deserved stature in the best of all tribes, the best of all parties, the best of all religions: the Adults.

Entropy, Interrupted

Revisiting the work of physicist Jeremy England, we're reminded that his new theory posits that the conflict between entropy (the idea that the universe tears down order to create chaos) and life (the continuous build-up of evermore-complicated organic molecules and increasingly complex living organisms) is solved by a simple principle: it is the nature of matter to *spread energy*.

At the most extreme macro level, this makes perfect sense and is observably happening: since the Big Bang, energy has been pouring out into the universe like spilled water on a kitchen floor, finding every possible path to every possible destination. Like kitchen furniture, the specks of matter in the universe - planets, comets, asteroids, interstellar dust - block and deflect that energy. And, as kitchen furniture gets wet, matter in the path of energy soaks it up.

Per Einstein, we know that matter itself - including us! - is simply condensed energy. That condensation is nothing more than an incidental consequence of certain thermodynamic conditions in certain places in space. Our planet, its atmosphere, its water, all the life on it - including us! - are an incidental mass of condensed energy, no different than all the other chunks of not-quite-energy dancing around stars and wandering through cold interstellar space.

Except...

Here on this particular planet, things are a little bit different.

Spreading Energy

First, a bit more of England: his team observes in their published papers that the Spread Energy imperative, elegant and simple, is observable everywhere in Nature. So ubiquitous is it, when sought out, that it is clearly the rule, not the exception: the properties of matter, both living and non-, all give service to this imperative. The Spread Energy imperative appears to be the very nature of Nature (though the theory is not yet proven).

England appears as a character in Dan Brown's novel *Origin*, which provides examples of natural organization that promotes entropy: simple objects, like snowflakes - frozen water - which spontaneously form complex shapes to most efficiently distribute light and heat. They cannot *not* do so. Quartz displays similar properties – elegant organization of non-living matter, optimized to radiate energy efficiently.

Origin's examples include weather, which can be characterized as complex systems that optimize to dissipate energy in the atmosphere, from the pressure-relieving vortex of a tornado to the electrical discharge of a lightning bolt, dispelling the structured ganging of charged particles in a thundercloud.

Even the simple mechanisms of life demonstrate England's principle – and life turns out to be matter's best innovation yet, when it comes to the spreading of energy. Photosynthesis, *Origin* points out, is a marvelous example: a tree absorbs a steady stream of sunlight, absconding with some of it to extend and replicate itself, while dissipating the remainder as infrared radiation: increased entropy.

And as for DNA, the engine of organic replication – it, too, exists in the service of entropy: a forest, for instance, can dissipate far more energy than a single tree.

If all of this is how Nature really works - and it appears increasingly likely - then England's Spread Energy principle explains how organic molecules came to be, and why increasing complexity is their rule: what we call life is in fact just another expression of matter's inherent imperative to get out of energy's way, and to exploit energy in that endeavor.

(This new feature of the universe, by the way, closes the final gap that God has been filling since Darwin. With the tendency of organic molecules to form under certain thermodynamic conditions, and for those molecules to form increasingly complex structures, the origin of life is now explained in full - the need for a 'Creator' has finally expired. The question, "How do living systems arise from non-living matter?" has finally been answered, if England is correct. This is a major theme of *Origin*.)

Physicists have already skipped ahead to the end of the universe's book: in the last pages of the final chapter, it will experience 'heat death' - the final cessation of all energy exchange, as there will eventually be no remaining thermodynamic fuel for entropic processes. England's model not only supports this long-accepted conclusion - it helps explain it.

Between now and the death of the universe, per England, the energy that it contains will continue to spread relentlessly - and all the specks of condensation, all the matter, will inadvertently interrupt that spread, catching and trapping energy in the process. And that captured energy will cause the substance of that matter, the cold particles that cause it to be, to rally for its release, scrambling to combine with other particles in whatever way will promote the energy.

There is no other outcome. All of physics, all of reality, all the laws of Nature yet discovered, bow in service to this unceasing agenda. ...including, again, us.

The Last Resort

It is matter's job to get out of energy's way, however it can, as fast as it can. It is energy's job, when it attempts to spread and finds itself thwarted by intervening matter, to infiltrate that matter and do what it must to push through; and, if possible, cause that matter to return to its own natural state – to *become* energy, when conditions are favorable.

If England's inspiration causes us to reconsider the origins and purpose of life, how does that inform our opinions about whether there's any more of it out there in the universe?

If anything, the England Imperative - *Spread Energy!* - makes the universe an easier place to understand. We are already very clear on the laws of thermodynamics, and so the imperative isn't exactly a sharp turn. But it casts a new light on our assumption that since we live in a universe where the elements of life are abundant, given uncounted billions of opportunities to occur, life will certainly make many appearances.

The England Imperative strongly suggests that life is only going to arise in places where matter can't easily spread energy in a less complicated way. Energy, interrupted by matter, will push through the path of least resistance; matter, organizing to optimize energy's quest, will only become as complex as it needs to be to accomplish that mission. Put another way, life – as the most complex of matter's mechanisms for dissipating energy – is a last resort.

A wickedly simple expression of the England Imperative might be an asteroid orbiting a star - composed of pure iron, let's say, and spinning slowly. The area of the asteroid facing the star will absorb energy from the star, then shed it into cold space as it rotates. It is, at most, a very temporary interruption of energy's journey to where. Nothing as intricate as life is necessary for the asteroid to perform its essential energy hand-off.

Even if the asteroid contained the elements of life, it wouldn't matter: because the thermodynamic system of the asteroid is so simple and performs so efficiently, nothing else is needed - and the additional conditions we know to be necessary for life are absent, in any case.

But an amazing thing happens when we begin to add those conditions: we begin to see direct parallels between the conditions required for life and the complexity of the energy capture of the place where it can take root. Put another way, a celestial body of great thermodynamic complexity and a planet that has conditions friendly to the emergence of life are one and the same.

The more thermodynamically complex the planet, the greater its friendliness to the emergence of life.

Using Earth as our only real baseline, we can observe that even with its staggeringly complex thermodynamic systems, life took its sweet time developing here. Once it did, it began doing its job - *spreading energy!* - and it is no great undertaking to chart the changes in the thermodynamics of the Earth in parallel with the increasing complexity of its emerging biosphere. What had to happen for such a system to emerge was for the planet's thermodynamic complexity to occur in the first place.

Let's examine that complexity briefly.

Complexities

The most famous of the characteristics of a life-bearing planet is that it be a Goldilocks planet. This means the planet exists in its parent star's *circumstellar habitable zone* (CHZ) - not too close, not too far away - so that its surface can support liquid water. The not-too-close/not-too-far, then, translates to not-too-hot/not-too-cold, in terms of surface temperature.

To have liquid water on its surface, the planet must have atmospheric pressure to hold it in place - and to retain an atmosphere heavy enough for that kind of pressure, it must be impervious to solar winds, which would ordinarily strip away the atmosphere of a planet so close to its star. Earth passes this test (while, for instance, Mars does not), possessing a rotating liquid nickel-iron core (a natural dynamo) that gives the planet a solar radiation-repelling magnetic field. [Venus possesses only a sparse magnetic field, yet holds an atmosphere far denser than Earth's; even so, the consequences of this are life-prohibitive - the solar winds are indeed eroding its upper atmosphere, and that activity has been depleting the planet of low-mass hydrogen and oxygen ions for billions of years, ridding it of all the water it may have originally possessed.]

A planet must also rotate at a certain pace - fast enough to pass heat in the course of rotation such that the surface water doesn't ever get hot enough to boil outright, but slowly enough that some of it evaporates, in order to carry water to land by way of clouds. And its mass must be such that it creates a gravitational field wherein life, once it forms, is secure without being crushed.

These characteristics, in combination, put a planet in an entirely different thermodynamic class than a simple iron asteroid. As the planet rotates, it will catch and release heat, as the asteroid does - but with liquid water on its surface and a gentle thermal cycle, vast amounts of energy will nonetheless be trapped to endlessly cycle between land, sea, and air.

The endless cycling of energy creates for Earth an England problem: the matter contained within this huge thermal vista must further organize and complexify in the service of spreading it. Snowflakes happen; tornadoes spring up.

But even that isn't enough, thermodynamically, to create a need for an energy-spreading mechanism as complex as life.

The Earth traps energy above and beyond storing it in air and water and rocks: it shakes and stirs it like a bartender.

Earth spins on an axis, as all planets do. But the spin of the Earth literally has a twist: the planet's axis is tilted, rather than perpendicular to the solar plane. This is, of course, the basis of the seasons. And the seasons are, almost by definition, the gradual shifting of energy from one planetary region to another, in yet another endless thermal cycle, as it revolves around the sun.

And the shaking and stirring goes further still: even more thermodynamically important than the Earth's axial tilt, perhaps, is the gravitational effects of its oversized moon. At one-quarter the size of the Earth itself, the moon is by far the largest satellite of a planet known to exist, ratio-wise.

The consequence, of course, is the intense tidal forces it brings: the moon churns the planet's oceans, generating still more energy to be trapped in liquid matter. The Earth's oceans are literally vast reservoirs of energy.

Now the complexity of the Earth has it working overtime to spread energy, because there are so many constantly-interacting systems trapping and re-trapping energy within - and new mechanisms for spreading it must rally to the task. Elements must combine, molecules become more intricate. New systems must interrupt the existing ones, to push against the bulwark of this tense equilibrium.

Now Life emerges. Self-replicating energy couriers of microscopic size, dedicated to scooping up energy from the environment and radiating it out, with far more intensity than a snowflake and far more intricacy than a tornado. A whole new chapter begins, as life interrupts not only the equilibrium of Earth's dancing thermodynamic systems, but their chemical composition as well. Carbon dioxide, methane, and other heat-trapping molecules of the sort that are currently broiling Venus become essential players in this disruption, paradoxically leveraged to solve the problem they themselves create. If Earth was a complicated story before, now it's a James Joyce novel.

And the supreme complexity in the system – life! – serves to introduce new complications that perpetuate the precarious balance between thermodynamic systems, even as they succeed in spreading energy to high heaven. We have named those complications *flora* and *fauna*.

In its simplest forms, life is a marvelous dissipative adaptation; even in an incarnation as simple as algae, it absorbs and redistributes energy, using some of it to replicate itself and thereby increase its utility, thus contributing to entropy. And as we've noted above, more sophisticated forms - land-based plant life being a great example - are even more impactful, turning an empty expanse of heat-absorbing dirt into a sprawling, infrared-radiant entropy engine that will spread and spread.

Algae and plants - all forms of life, really – are reorganizations of matter in the service of energy redistribution. But unlike snowflakes and tornadoes and other transitory, one-off mechanisms, living organisms themselves take on the role of energy trap: they collect more energy than their raw materials would, if dissociated, and apply that energy to the purposes of entropy.

And when we get to animal life, the England Imperative gets more creative still: animals don't just absorb solar energy, exploit it, then redistribute it; animals can capture and trap the energy *of other living things*, other energy traps. They extract the energy of other plants and animals. In this process, entropy is served on yet another level: the animal consumption of other forms of life, in releasing that life's energy, breaks it down - *order into chaos* - entropy, once again.

This stupendous innovation is remarkable enough in itself. But it gives rise to one of the most unusual features of the Earth's biosphere: the thermodynamically precarious swap of gases between plant life and animal life. Respiration is experienced by plants and animals alike, with plants emitting oxygen and animals emitting carbon dioxide - a complementary accommodation that benefits both, keeping both kingdoms of life in equilibrium. If either kingdom were to vanish from the Earth, the other would be hard-pressed to survive.

And it grows more complicated still: as animal life has taken the lead as both the premiere redistributor of energy on the planet and its most explicit and dedicated hoarder, it simultaneously (and unwittingly) contributes to the planet's entropy interruption: carbon dioxide and methane, the two gases animals emit, are themselves energy traps. They capture and retain heat; when expelled into the atmosphere, they cause the atmosphere itself to hoard more energy than before.

Repurposed

In hindsight, the emergence of life here on Earth seems inevitable; but the take-home point is that the Earth is as thermodynamically different even from planets of comparable size as an internal combustion engine is from a wind-up watch. We are children of the most unlikely of planets. To say that Earth is one in a billion would be almost certainly understate. And, as a side note, the implications of the England Imperative make the ubiquity of complex life in the universe a *very* distant possibility. It is highly improbable that the universe is teeming with life – which makes the life here on Earth all the more precious.

We can, if England's theory proves true, employ it as a predictive tool as we venture out into the universe: encountering new worlds, we would estimate the likelihood of finding life or something like it based on the world's observable energy traps, its thermodynamic complexity. The more straightforward its energy transfer, the less need for an energy dissipation system as intricate as life.

Here on Earth itself, however, it would have been impossible, given the planet's staggering energy burden, for life *not* to have emerged: our planet is a clogged energy sink, capturing the radiation of the sun and hoarding it shamelessly, passing it from system to system, releasing to the night only what it absolutely can't permanently ensnare during the day.

The conclusion is simple and profound and deeply disturbing: we are products of entropy interruption. And our purpose, as far as the universe is concerned, is the spreading of energy. We are here only because in this universe, elements combine in the way that most efficiently pushes energy along, and our particular molecules happen to be situated in the mother of all energy traps.

Any purpose beyond that transcends that of the universe - and is entirely ours to define.

Stars are the forges of energy, emitting it endlessly in an effort to warm the void; planets are interrupters of that entropy; and we are, ironically, planetary disrupters.

We are both agents of and disruptors of entropy. We, the highest form of life, having emerged as reality's champions of energy dissipation, are uniquely positioned to seize the reins of energy distribution – and have already begun doing so, in the order we have created for ourselves out of the raw materials of the Earth. As self-directed entropy engines, we can use our power to increase the interruption of entropy in the service of order, redirecting the dissipation of energy in a manner that complements our industry as the gases of plants and animals complement one another. We can refine our powers of disruption, redirect the role of matter, and leverage entropy's chaos as a means, not an end.

We can, put simply, repurpose the universe.

Origin, indeed...

Man's Best EON

Neil deGrasse Tyson, in his new version of *Cosmos*, tells of how humans domesticated dogs. About 32,000 years ago, we occupied Europe, and local wolves watched us at night from the shadows as we ate our meat around a roaring fire - a fire the wolves deeply feared.

But a few wolves, Tyson explained, were more curious than afraid: they approached, cautiously, more interested in exploring the situation and understanding these newcomers than in the safety of cold shadow.

In other words, these were EON wolves - more curious than afraid, more focused on opportunity than threat - and they were rewarded with the scraps from the fire. They learned that by approaching cautiously, and not putting forth threatening behaviors, they would receive superior-tasting warm meat as reward.

Thus began a partnership - the human and the domesticated dog - which persists to this day.

But the story does not end there. In 2009, archaeologists unearthed the canine skulls that demonstrated the speciation from the wolf that led us to this new information (Pat Shipman writes about this in his book "The Invaders") and it in turn explained the rapid overthrow of the Neandertal in Europe (who had maintained a foothold for hundreds of thousands of years, since long before the emergence of Homo sapiens); we out-hunted and out-survived the Neandertal within a comparative handful of generations, because we had, as allies, cooperative partners whose sense of smell was vastly superior to our own. We won the hominin race, largely due to our cooperation with the EON wolf.

There are lessons in there somewhere...

I Was Right!

I was right! is the refrain of the arrogant;
I was wrong! is the coda of the humble.

I was right! is the wail of the persecuted;
I was wrong! is the testimony of the liberated.

I was right! is the mantra of the secretly insecure;
I was wrong! is the cornerstone of the truly confident.

I was right! is a path to stunted thinking;
I was wrong! is a path to broader thinking.

I was right! is the membership card of the echo chamber;
I was wrong! is the escape key.

I was right! is the shout of the defiant child;
I was wrong! is the confession of the emerging adult.

Still More Empathy

We've made many mentions of the role that Empathy plays in the formation of our social biases and behaviors. Trump's latest breathtaking tirade once again teases out the very fundamental fact that most of the discord we experience in the world emerges from our collisions with one another over how we view other human beings and what assumptions about them we cling to.

Empathy, in its infuriating variability, is at the core of our greatest successes and our most abhorrent failures. It is the enabler of unity. It is the foundation of achievement. It is the basis. of inequality. It is the driver of war.

Some have a great deal of it, some have little or none. And that's why we experience these staggering fails and shocking moments. That's why our politics and policies are so unstable.

But the toughest fact of all is this: how much or how little empathy any individual has is regulated by the amount of tissue they have in a very specific part of their brain - and they were born that way.

We can disapprove of low-empathy policies, we can find low-empathy statements revolting, we can want low-empathy decision-makers out of power - but we can't hate those with low-empathy for having very little empathy. They don't choose to be that way. Hating them is no different than hating people for being black or gay or female.

Under the Sheets

When I was a kid, growing up immersed in Midwestern Fundamentalism, we had to be pretty innovative in seeking out fun.

We spent an astounding amount of time actually sitting in church – far, far more than any contemporary families do today: Sunday morning service, Sunday evening service, Wednesday evening service, weekly youth group, weekly Bible study, choir practice. You can imagine.

To pass this time, we had a number of games tucked away, many of which were filled with sort of reckless daring that causes Flick to freeze his tongue to the light pole in *A Christmas Story*. The best of these, we would play during the services in the sanctuary – during the sermon.

My father was the pastor, so this was all the more daring for me personally: if I were to laugh out loud during the sermon, my father would stop preaching, call me out in front of the entire congregation, and make me come sit on the front pew.

The all-time greatest game: Under the Sheets.

This was back in the days before praise choruses, when the pews held hymnals filled with old worship songs. To play, you just picked up a hymnal, opened it randomly, and added the words "…Under the Sheets" to whatever title presented. Then you had to try not to laugh out loud.

The pacesetters, of course, you can guess without even tracking down a hymnal. "How Great Thou Art" leads the field, with "Count Your Blessings" and "I Need Thee Every Hour" hovering just beneath.

"Abide with Me", "O Happy Day" and "All Praise to Thee" rank high, with "How Sweet Are the Tidings" and "Thine Be the Glory" garnering strong honorable mentions.

The older one gets, of course, the funnier the game becomes, as dawning sexual awareness opens up new layers of entendre. "Hold Fast till I Come" is more than a 14-year-old can stand, while "Have

Thine Own Way" and "I Surrender All" strongly suggest a certain role-playing supplication (the UK offers the variation "Brother, Let Me Be Your Servant").

"We Gather Together" and "Blest Be the Tie That Binds" border on outright kink.

As we grew up, hymns faded away as praise choruses took hold, offering an entirely new canon. Bill Gaither got this rolling with "He Touched Me", and the Christian music industry's annual refresh of content kept the hits rolling: "Draw Me Close to You" and "Amazing Love" were somewhat tame, but "He Has Made Me Glad" and "Worthy, You Are Worthy" would draw a snicker. "You Are So Good to Me" and "You Are My All in All" can be all the funnier depending on who's sitting next to you, and "I'm Forever Grateful" goes unspurned.

Myself, I'm old school – I always come home to the classics. So I'll leave it with my personal favorite: "O For a Thousand Tongues"...

Generation Z, Part III

Returning once again to my conversation with my teenage daughter – the conversation about how her generation differs so radically from the generations preceding – I was struck by one additional point she made.

Her generation isn't growing up, heading off to college, settling down and having kids with anywhere near the enthusiasm of their forebears.

They are, instead, staying in Mom and Dad's basement, getting a low-end job, and living much as they did before.

Why is that? I asked my daughter.

Remember that her two previous points – that Generation Z has been equipped with a top-heavy world model at an early age, plus an unusual sense of 24/7 inclusion – were based on the fact that she and her peers were the first generation to grow up completely within the Internet. It turns out that in her mind, that has negative consequences as well.

Why, she asked me back, *would I and the rest of my generation charge out into the world? There's nothing out there for us.*

Wow.

That just about broke my heart.

Why do you feel that way, I wondered? The very Internet that caused you all to grow up so fast and provide you with built-in community is also the greatest single source of opportunity human beings have ever created!

She shook her head sadly.

No, she told me, *the Internet sends back just the opposite message: whatever my goals, whatever my aspirations, I can never be more than mediocre; the Internet is an endless parade of countless people doing what I dream of doing, only doing it far better than I ever could.*

And I thought of a Vonnegut quote (from his novel *Bluebeard*):

"A moderately gifted person who would have been a community treasure a thousand years ago has to give up, has to go into some other line of work, since modern communications put him or her into daily competition with nothing but world's champions..."

As I listened to my daughter, I realized that no matter how much encouragement her family and friends might give her, it might never offset the impact of all the world's champions on parade, over phone and tablet and laptop, in endless loops.

My daughter deserves her dreams. She deserves not just encouragement to match the cold water buckets of cybernews, but a platform of her own in that venue.

That's something I can work on, something I owe her. We all owe all of our children that – we created this monster called the Internet, we willingly surrendered our time and energy and dopamine receptors to it, and in the process, intertwined it into our children's economic and creative future beyond any hope of extraction. We absolutely must take the next step: clean the damn thing up and infuse it with some purpose beyond meme-surfing and shopping convenience.

And that means a rethinking of our legacy.

We weren't thinking of our kids when we started browsing the Internet – we were just fascinated with all the cool shit there was out there.

We weren't thinking of our kids when we started putting our businesses and government online – we were just blown away at having to drive and use the phone less.

We weren't thinking of our kids when we started carrying supercomputers in our pockets, and substituting thumb-taps for conversations.

We weren't thinking of our kids when we started outsourcing our participation in community and public discourse to social media. We weren't thinking of our kids.

But now we look just over our shoulder, and there they are: tens of millions of them, all grown up and ready to inherit the earth – and uninterested in venturing out of the basement. Unmotivated to train for and undertake careers. Unmotivated to start families.

We need to rethink our legacy. Then we need to rebuild it. And the starting point is the asking of a very harsh question:

What have we done???

Eight Chickens

I recently went through a fried chicken phase. It became convenient for me to swing by the neighborhood grocery store, buy a recently fried, segmented chicken in a plastic tray, and take home an easy dinner and the next day's lunch.

This habit persisted probably longer than it should have, and came to a halt when I happened to arrive at the deli in time to see a new batch of fried chicken being prepared. The deli lady stood at a table next to a deep fryer, rolling chicken parts in batter, loading them into a wire basket, lowering them into boiling vegetable oil.

I realized, in horror, that the chicken parts were coming from plastic bags - and each bag was filled with the same part: a bag of wings, a bag of legs, a bag of thighs, a bag of breasts. Two of each would go into a plastic tray, summing up to a whole chicken.

But the reality is... eight chickens.

When I was taking home a tray of chicken, I was eating parts from eight separate chickens. The original chicken, when undergoing segmentation, was being distributed into a vast ocean of chicken parts, forever scattered. My dinner-and-next-day's-lunch tray was the final resting place of parts from eight different chickens.

This struck me as perverse. It's one thing to be a chicken on a family farm in a bygone time, and have your head chopped off in order to adorn the evening dinner table, to be ceremoniously and lovingly consumed by the family that raised you from a chick; it's quite another to be rended and randomized, launched into the anonymous abyss of family dinner roulette, subjected to the neighborhood deli's casual mass-production indignities. Imagine being the chicken, winding up on eight different dinner tables!

Bad for the chicken - but worse for me, taking home parts from eight different ones! Eight different chickens from eight different places; each with its own identity, its own story, their journeys curtailed by a cruel, common destiny - me. It's more guilt than I care to bear.

I left the deli in a troubled state of mind, resolving to end my callous dining practice. I would participate in this contemptuous carnage no longer. I found a drive-thru, got a bucket of hot wings, and headed home.

Nihilism

At its most simple, the word 'nihilism' refers to a belief that there is no inherent meaning to life and existence. Religions tend to revise the word to mean 'rejection of religion' or 'embrace of amorality', and this is 1) inaccurate, and 2) self-serving.

The argument that there is no 'inherent' meaning to human existence is easily supported; that we are a highly successful evolutionary branch of the great apes is at this point firmly established by the scientific evidence, and that puts humankind in the domain of nature - which exists for its own sake, not to fulfill any imagined purpose.

But this is not to say that nihilism can be extended to presume amorality - human morality, defined as a worldview and behavioral frame, fits within nature; as eusocial beings, our morality co-evolved with our brains, and exists for its own sake, as nature does - and has persisted as a consequence of its contribution to our collective survival.

The Real Problem

It's never been simpler to feel smug.

Seriously, it takes no effort whatsoever for those not in thrall to the Oval Office occupant - or what's left of the party that installed him – to feel superior, self-satisfied, full of oneself. The daily parade of hypocrisy, naked power grabs, moral turpitude, and all-out assault on institutions that have served and protected us for generations has a way of hardening our sense of rightness like cement. We peer down from our lofty ethical perch in disdain, fanning our righteous indignation to bonfire intensity, dead-certain that we are the good guys and they are not.

There is also a kind of implicit urgency in this smugness, a feeling that we are getting outraged and incensed in the service of a great cause – that our disapproval of and opposition to the behaviors of the encroaching Authoritarians is a summons to action, a noble clarion call. To the voting booth, everyone! There's no time to waste!

Don't get me wrong: yes, we are witnessing breathtaking hypocrisies almost hourly; yes, our most essential institutions are being undermined; yes, this is unquestionably moral turpitude at its turpitudiest. And yes, our smug sense of rightness is not without foundation.

But the embrace of that smugness is in itself every bit as dangerous as the waters we now tread, for it is smugness that gives rise to the Authoritarian in the first place.

In the broiling heat of these never-ending moments, our focus is seized by memes and clickbait headlines and sound bites, and we leap impulsively into the cockfight of this issue or that, opening fire on the immoral this or the unethical that, and demeaning the offender with relish. We've been called to battle, after all. Isn't this our moral duty?

We are embattled, yes, and we certainly do have a moral duty. But it would help enormously to shift our focus to the actual enemy.

Isn't that the guy in the Oval? Isn't that the GOP, the Republican leadership? Isn't all of this the struggle of Democracy against Authoritarianism? Again, yes. But we get nowhere fighting in a burning house; if we're going to truly push back against the Authoritarian, we need to understand where he comes from.

The problem is not the Oval Office occupant. It is not the GOP leadership. It is not those who voted for them. It is not conservatives, it is not Republicans.

The problem is not the partisan obsessions of the right. The problem is partisanism itself.

Partisanism is the institutionalization of smugness, the compartmentalization of righteousness. Partisanism is the self-lobotomizing of group thought, the systematic and intentional corruption of cooperation. Partisanism takes our most useful social potential and hijacks it in service of arbitrary tribes; it robs us of our broader human impulses, substituting confectionary vanities and illusory fulfillments.

Partisanism dismantles our superb capacity to achieve greater knowledge and wisdom and accomplishment when diverse minds join together. It dulls our thoughts, truncating the reach of our perception and understanding, limiting the depth and breadth of effective decision.

Worst of all, partisanism dilutes empathy. It diminishes the humanity of those outside the imaginary circles it generates, making it easier to tune them out and turn them away. It bestows undeserved credit upon the compliant and unfair debit upon the dissentient; it robs us of some of our own humanity as it obscures our view of the humanity in others. In short, it opens up a wound in each of us and actively obstructs its healing.

This is what we are really seeing around us right now: a growing diminishment of our ability to work together, when we most need to; a festering inability to truly address problems that are unraveling our social fabric; and a death of empathy, when empathy is our salvation.

It's not about the president, or the GOP, or conservative ideology; they just happen to have the stage at the moment. It's about how we cripple ourselves when we huddle into groups based on a single viewpoint, breathing in the affirmation and agreement, lazing in our inflatable certainties. Those groups, whatever their labels, all share these disabling features.

But there's one other feature of partisanism that we can ponder, and in the pondering, seek out hope.

Partisanism is a choice.

The Savanna Principle

Taking delight in the differences between human beings necessarily begins with enjoying them in the first place.

How this state is achieved and how it works, once achieved, are questions central to our understanding of human nature, and have been for thousands of years. Are human beings naturally competitive or cooperative? Are we instinctively wary of others, or inwardly welcoming? Are the answers to these questions the same today as they were 100,000 years ago, and if not, why not?

That human beings are the ultimate cooperators in the annals of life is beyond dispute: no other species comes close to having achieved what we achieve when we operate collectively, for good or ill. But what drives that cooperation? Economics? Improving our survival by controlling the environment? Tribal dynamics?

Satoshi Kanazawa, an evolutionary psychologist at the London School of Economics, had a different idea. In 2004, he proposed the Savanna Principle, which suggests that human beings remain adapted to the environment in which we evolved – central Africa – and that many of our modern-world dysfunction may be attributed to our inherent incompatibility with the environment we have created for ourselves. Our ancient hunger for sugars, for instance – a survival advantage in an environment protein-rich and sugar-poor, where quick-hit energy and immediate storage of ingested carbohydrates could be a huge benefit – is extremely detrimental to our health in the modern era, where all foods are plentiful and none of us are ever tasked with fleeing from large, fast predators.

We are already neck-deep in that general idea, but Kanazawa offers a wrinkle that we can add to our thinking. The wrinkle we now add is the dopamine *ding*, that rewarding little boost we feel in our brains when we solve a problem, eat a tasty meal, or have sex. Dopamine is our inner assurance that all is right with the world – and we can tie it to a further thought of Kanazawa's.

That idea posits that human tribes on the savanna faced an almost endless series of challenges, puzzles and problems beyond the ken of any individual – and that a human tribe could, collectively, thrive in such a world far better than an individual. This idea, which he crafted with Norman Li of Singapore Management University, was dubbed the Savanna Theory of Happiness – that the impulse modern humans feel to be around other humans is a holdover from our savanna days, when there was pleasure in facing the dangers of the world surrounded by other problem-solvers.

(A corollary to this idea is its explanatory force regarding high-IQ individuals, who prefer solitude to a far greater degree – because, the theory suggests, they are superb problem solvers on their own, with less need for the emotional relief of a surrounding tribe.)

When we fold the dopamine *ding* into that theory, we take a huge leap forward: we have a physical, genetically-linked attribute of human cognition (dopamine receptivity) that supports the idea of group selection, that cooperative human groups are subject to an evolutionary driver above the level of personal survival and gene transmission.

The Robots are Coming!

The androids of *Westworld* exist to please their users, whatever the cost. They are designed to be indistinguishable from human men and women in bed, are able to simulate desire, and to append all the expected peripheral behaviors to sexual acts, whether in romance or rape. They are intended to give their users whatever pleasure is asked of them, without conditions, without consequences. And they are so life-like, they believe they are alive.

Fifty years earlier, *Star Trek* had gone down the same path, when the wealthy recluse Flint, a man 6,000 years old and beyond the range of ordinary human love, built with his knowledge and wealth an equally immortal partner: the android Rayna, who - like the women of *Westworld* - did not even realize she was an artificial person.

And then there are the *Stepford Wives*.

These are profound stories that inspire profound questions, and we'll get to them. But in doing so, we must note that they are no longer just stories.

In 2016, a Chinese AI engineer named Zheng Jiajia faced a disheartening dilemma: at 31, he was under pressure from family and friends to marry, but had found that he simply could not compete in the real world. He was unable to attract a mate, possibly due to his country's one-child-per-family policy, which has led to the practice of sex-selective abortion, resulting in more males than females in the general population.

Applying his professional skills to his problem, Zheng crafted a partner for himself, just as the fictional Flint did. He literally built himself a woman.

Naming her Ying-Ying, he even went so far as to marry her in an unofficial ceremony attended by his mother and friends. He even wrapped her head in a red cloth, as tradition called for.

Ying-Ying cannot walk. But she can speak a little, can recognize images - and Zheng takes her to work with him each day. She will someday be given upgrades, Zheng has said, so that she can do chores.

This is a bit of a jaw drop, but the truth is that sex dolls - life-size silicone simulacrums of human women and men, with whom actual human women and men can have sex - have been with us for a few years now, and have become quite the luxury item. As futurists and technologists have been assuring us for some time, sex robots are the inevitable next step - and they are beginning to appear.

The difference between doll and robot amounts to responsiveness: a sex doll does not react to the mating acts of its user; a sex robot is able to see and hear the user, and offer spoken responses. Those responses are limited, of course; but even a simulated sigh or ecstatic outcry is enough to make a huge difference for some. And the most sophisticated models are able to learn about their human partners, to a very limited degree, and offer a very limited range of conversation, making them even more user-friendly.

Doll or robot, these sex commodities are, unsurprisingly, deeply controversial.

But they are also inevitable, and will change us more and more as we develop and improve them.

The controversies are what you'd expect: Sex with a robot or doll is the same as cheating! They are no substitute for true intimacy! They will dehumanize us! They could be hacked, making them blackmailers or assassins for the hackers! The list goes on.

Alice Vaughn of the *Two Girls, One Mic* podcast, doesn't see a problem:

"There are a myriad of reasons why someone would want to purchase a sex doll," she said on *The Thinking Atheist* podcast in 2019. "The most common that you're going to hear are persons who say, 'I'm just tired of being alone'... 'I don't want the head games'... 'My spouse and I have a sexless relationship'... 'With dolls, I can be myself.' These are people who either are in struggling relationships where they're not being sexually fulfilled, or they're people who just had a number of experiences with others that just didn't pan out, and they're frustrated. And I can understand and relate to that, frankly. I think most people can: if you just have shitty relationship after relationship, wouldn't something that gives a lot of the appeal of a human being, that might resolve the frustration, wouldn't that be appealing? to at least give you some release?"

She offered other reasons. "There's also the flexibility and submissiveness, allowing you to try any sexual stunt without cheating or risk of an STD or STI. You can potentially use a sex doll as a couple without any judgment, do a threesome, in the case of failing marriages, or even losing a partner, which is very hurting and can take time, you know, before going into another relationship."

Vaughn's optimism is shared by many. The company Real Doll believes its male love robots will become utterly suitable and desired substitutes for actual men, not only able to speak and listen, but to offer up a stored narrative - a personal history! - and personality traits that are compatible with their owner. The relationship, the company claims, will even be unique and, therefore, special. Put another way, sex robots are poised not only to fill a niche market, but to one day enter the mainstream.

Let's think about how all of this is going to play out.

First, let's remember that we're talking about technology, and it's technology that is poised to become very, very popular. Today a quality sex doll can cost $5,000 or more, and a sex robot up to ten times that much - but that cost will fall to the barest fraction of that amount, when sex robots are mass-produced, just as the cost of any new technology drops when it goes viral. Digital calculators initially cost hundreds of dollars; today, you can buy one for pocket change.

Then let's consider whether Vaughn is right about the "toy" factor: no matter how lifelike, a sex robot is ultimately an appliance, just an ultra-sophisticated vibrator or dildo or fleshlight with Siri built in. Unless you watch *The 700 Club*, that means zero-judgment sex, pregnancy- and STD-free, for many if not most who desire it.

As prices fall and availability increases, these robots will begin taking up residence in homes - and, inevitably, dorms, college fraternity and sorority houses. They will become party participants. Given their accountability-free nature, they could usher in a sharp increase in selective group sex. That will certainly tilt our cultural sensitivities, for better or worse.

They will make homosexual sex easier to explore, also consequence- and shame-free, for those who are naturally inclined toward it. That, too, will significantly impact our social frame - probably for the better.

As Vaughn predicts, synthetic partners will be invited into real relationships. Couples who might never even think about including another human in their private intimacy, even though they desire it, could easily integrate an artificial one.

Sex robots could - and certainly will - be used to teach sexual technique, a desperately-needed social function. They could - and certainly will - replace human brothels, and may be positioned to decimate human trafficking.

On the downside, it is easy to imagine a person in a relationship with another person abandoning that relationship, if challenges arise, for the ease of an artificial relationship with a synthetic one. Or turning to the robot, rather than the partner, leaving the partner still in the relationship but sexually ignored. It is also easy to imagine the anything-goes nature of human-robot sex bringing down shame and judgment upon a partner who is unable to comply with a robot user's over-the-top desires.

Then there's the door that might open in some people who are monogamous, once they've tasted of silicone promiscuity, indulging that taste back among human partners, to their own detriment.

All of this isn't just possible; all of it, every last bit of it, is inevitable. All of it.

And there's another thing we can be absolutely certain of: as sex robots become ubiquitous, integrated into the marketplace and ultimately embedded as a permanent feature of society, the market will demand that they grow more and more sophisticated, more and more lifelike, as their economic success attracts the resources to drive the technology forward. It will, you can be certain, happen at astonishing speed. We can even anticipate that the evolution of androids in the human story will be driven, not by their potential role as workers and labor-savers, but as lovers.

And a final thought, as certain as those above: the introduction of artificial sex partners into the human equation, despite whatever benefits accrue, ultimately won't change the one thing that needs changing.

We were, as a species, sexually crippled before they came along. We have been for many thousands of years. Patriarchy and inequality gave us misogyny, to the horrific detriment of both women and men, tearing our social intimacy asunder, ripping us apart, depriving us of the deep fellowship that kept us alive for three million moons. We'll still be crippled later, regardless of how sex robots evolve and how we integrate with them. What's broken inside us has made human intimacy less than it should be, as far back as memory goes - and robots can never fix that.

Choosed

We don't - we *can't* - "choose" our sexuality, or who we're attracted to: those are complex nervous system responses that live below the level of conscious thought (do we "choose" our nervous systems?).

But there are many other things we don't "choose." We don't "choose" our food preferences; our senses of smell and taste are highly individual, and they respond without our conscious guidance. Do they change? Sometimes, but only sometimes, and then very gradually, over time - with repeated exposure to new input.

Likewise, we don't "choose" our emotional biases or our "beliefs," which are based on our emotional responses. These bubble up from beneath the level of conscious thought, and at best we rationalize them intellectually. These, too, can change over time, with new experience and input - but only over time. We can't simply decide, Oh, I think I'll change my beliefs today!

So, you know, let's cut ourselves - and each other - a little slack...

A Function of the Brain

Empathy is a function of the brain, dependent upon the amount of tissue our genes dole out in this or that corner of our skulls. We are socially trained in how to express it, of course, but how much we actually *feel* is not up to us. It's how we were born.

Low-empathy people cluster together into social groups to form and support world-views that conform to low empathy.

High-empathy people cluster together into social groups to form and support world-views that conform to high empathy.

Do you see the problem?

The Choice Was This...

- fill them with religion, conformity, predestined roles, or

- fill them with ideas, art, and humor, and see what happens...

Hope and Fear

The hope of an economy increasingly data-driven, where the manipulations of the dominant break against the wall of a steadily-bolstered reality, is that reliance upon analytics will restore empiricism and sober reliance upon fact to their rightful place in our social and economic deliberations.

Everywhere this trend manifests, good things happen; bad decisions and the slick voices of those spouting them fade.

It's all about outcomes, in the end, as any real capitalist will tell you. You're not buying star players, you're buying base hits. The decision-maker who gets that wins the game, in the end - and so it must be, in the end, with nations, as smaller and weaker and less resource-rich countries around us set about modifying their economies into improvements upon our own.

The fear? That they, not we, will win the game in the end...

Vectors

Statistics serve us by providing accurate description of what we cannot observe directly and personally.

Here's a critical lesson: obtaining the accurate vector of a statistic is far more important than obtaining the accurate value of a statistic. Example: when I was in the 4th grade, the global human population was three billion. Today, a generation later, it is seven billion.

But our statistic – global human population - is more than two numbers separated by time; the vector, the speed and direction of the value, give us two more numbers – more important numbers. How fast is the statistic's value changing? And in what direction?

If both of the value numbers are high by even an entire billion, but the vector is accurate, then the Oh Shit of the statistic remains (in fact, it becomes even worse: if the numbers are two billion and six billion, and the vector is correct, then the net rate of increase is greater). The values give us isolated moments; the vector tells us that the human population is increasing far too quickly.

If the values are off, but the vector is accurate, the actual *information* conveyed by my statistic nonetheless has meaning - it retains its importance. If the numbers are accurate, but the vector is off (for instance, if I think the value of a statistic is on the decline, when it is in fact fluctuating, with a net gain), then my statistic is conveying the *opposite* of its true meaning.

Statistics show us the world as it is; but more importantly, they show us how it is changing. That's where our attention needs to be.

Hello, Babies!

Hello, babies!

Here I stand, in early morning, staring through a large window at about thirty of you – all newborns, all healthy, all beautiful!

None of you are mine, but I examined the brains of three of you over the past two hours, as part of my graduate studies. My work here is done! And I must soon head back to campus, but I thought I would stop in and say hello first.
Six feet to my left, a small girl is lifted up by her father so that she can see one of you, presumably her new sibling. She is very excited!

Inside the nursery, most of you are immersed in post-delivery slumber, like your nearby mommies. A few of you have been here for a day or more. One or two of you are crying, a few more are squirmy and restless. Three nurses calmly and skillfully monitor you all, tending you as needed. But mostly the scene is calm.

Let me describe you, babies, as I'm seeing you right now.

The pink and the blue you're wrapped in are roughly equal, as I'd expect. Four of you are brown. Most of you look like Winston Churchill, though I also spotted a couple of J. Edgar Hoovers and a Lyndon Johnson. And, I think, a Newt Gingrich.

You brown babies, well, you're in for a rough ride. You should be proud of your skins, because as far as human babies go, you're in the overwhelming majority: there have been about 100 billion of us born over the past 300,000 years, and of those, at least 90 billion were the same color as you! But, alas, you are being born into a country where it's the other way around: only one baby in 10 here is the same color as you, and so you are in for a less happy life.

Those of you brown babies with penises are overwhelmingly likely to be denied the opportunities of the white babies around you. You will only get an education if your parents have a lot of money. The legal system considers you guilty until proven innocent, simply because you are brown. You are more likely to be considered dangerous by a policeman, and shot dead for no good reason, except being brown.

The non-brown babies around you will be trained from this moment on to view you with suspicion. You will live lives of deep stress, simply because you are not accepted by the society that is (at this moment, anyway) keeping you warm and safe. You penis-bearers, you're likely to die earlier than the white boy babies around you, because you are more likely to experience stress-induced heart disease; and you penis-free brown babies, you are likely to have your own babies too soon, simply because you are brown and stressed, and that will make their lives – and yours! - all the more difficult.

You made it this far because your mommies decided to carry you to term, and because nature did not intervene with a do-over. In most cases, that was a good decision – but for about six of you, maybe not so much. Though you are, at this moment, as healthy and as smart and as bursting with potential as all the other babies around you, you have been born into poverty. Your mommies and daddies do not have as much money as the mommies and daddies of the other babies here.

For many decades, here in the country of your birth, those who lead us and make our decisions have provided for you, even so; they considered you just as important, just as beautiful and filled with potential as your better-off neighbors here, and so they made sure that your parents' circumstances did not prevent you from getting the nutrition and medical care and education that it takes to grow up happy and healthy in this country. As a result, you are children of the healthiest, best-educated generation in this country's history.

However, all of that is changing. New people are in charge, and they see you differently. They do not see you poor babies as being worthy of all that. They see your mommies and daddies as lazy and unmotivated, as though their poverty was their own fault, because they do not work hard enough. I know, because I was given paperwork on all of you for my study, that the opposite is true: the poorest mommies and daddies among you work the most hours a week, but they are paid far less for their work. This is because the same people who do not think you should have assistance from the society that is here to nurture you, and who think your mommies and daddies are lazy, also think that your parents should not be allowed to bargain for their compensation collectively (because that practice is inconvenient to those in power - not surprisingly, them).

For these reasons, poor babies, I am sorry to say that your prospects are not so good.

Now let me say a word to those of you without penises.

As a grown-up with a penis, I address you not from experience but as a bearer of knowledge. Though, as you lie here, the only difference between you and your little brothers is the color of your blankets, you will be treated very differently, all the same. Your brains are the equal of your brothers (I know, because I just examined them!); your creativity and insight and raw talents are all the equal of theirs; and your stamina and ability to integrate information and, in most cases, your empathy, frankly put your tiny brothers to shame. If you were being born into a world that the penis-bearers worked to make fair and equitable for all, then you would be offered all the opportunity that will fall upon your brothers. But, alas, you're being born into a very different world.

As progressive as this country is, your mommies only recently received the right to sue for sexual harassment, or keep their jobs if they were going to become a mommy. And many of your grandmommies couldn't own a credit card, and your great-grandmommies couldn't vote. These things have changed, but if you are raped, or harassed in the workplace or otherwise sexually mistreated, the legal system will, by default, assume you are lying and that your attacker is telling the truth.

And despite your brains and talent and insight and stamina, you can look forward to being paid 20 percent less for your lack of a penis.

Finally, as I consider you all as the products of sex, rather than the practitioners you will all one day become, I must sadly inform you pink-blanketed babies that, while you have the same potential to grow into healthy, fulfilled sexual beings with capacities for passion and bonding and happiness equal to your brothers, you are destined to be shamed and demeaned for your desires, treated as disposable conveniences by the culture and media you are entering, rather than as the self-actualized treasures you have every reason to become.

Unfortunately, it doesn't end there: two of you pinks and two blues will find yourselves attracted, not to the opposite gender, but to your own. You'll be at some middle school party and someone will approach, and you'll get all nervous and tingly and forget how to talk. That's sexual attraction, as experienced in middle school. You won't have any say over this – we don't pick and choose who we're attracted to, our nervous systems decide for us. It's a curiosity of your particular brains and the ratio of hemisphere volume (remember, I was just there!). Just go with it!

But be wary – there are those in this unfortunate world who will label you perverts and sinners for this natural aspect of your existence, insisting that you did choose your preference and that you are perverts. These people are ignorant, self-righteous, and ultimately afraid of those who are different (and they are the same people who look down on brown babies and pink blanket babies). They will call for your death. They will not bake you cakes.

Ignore them as best you can. Many, many of us know that they are the problem, not you – and we've got your backs!

And now a word or two to all of you, penises and skin color aside:

Up until now, the lot of you could look forward to a number of things. You could count on the right to have a say in who is in power here in this country. You had the right to protection of your earnings. You had a government that would look out for your rights and safety and well-being, over and above those who have a great deal of money. Best of all, you had a firewall between you and poverty, especially in your old age.

Alas, there are now thousands of politicians, and tens of millions of your fellow citizens, who are working very hard to see to it that you have none of those things anymore – that the rights of those with large amounts of money take precedence over yours. It doesn't look good for any of you, frankly, and that is to our collective shame, for you are the first generation of children in this nation to face such collective disdain. However, though these people who don't have your little backs are out there in great force, there are even more – far more – people in this country who believe that you are our most precious resource, that you are inherently deserving of the best healthcare and a great education and equal opportunity and a strong, stable economy and clean air and water and a long, healthy life, with safeguards in place to protect you from life's twists and turns and speed-bumps.

Well, babies, my studies await, and I must away! I will leave you with one final thought, quoting one of my favorite authors, from whom I'll pass along the only rule that he knew of:

God damn it, you've got to be kind...

The Suppression of Cognitive Type

When like minds cluster together, uniformity of opinion, rhetoric and worldview results. Decisions and problem-solving are by rote, new information is seldom welcomed, and individual thought and contemplation begin atrophy.

When cognitive diversity appears, decisions and problem-solving become dynamic, new information is essential, and individual thought and contemplation are stimulated.

But what happens when an individual is bound to a social group based on like-mindedness, yet the individual is not of like mind? What happens to the fish out of water, surrounded by many minds that are uniform in their difference from the fish?

It's hard to imagine a worse fate: to see the world clearly in a way that makes personal sense, and to be embedded among people who see everything very differently, is a personal hell of formidable proportions. It's a flavor of loneliness that must be worse than actually being alone?

Why would a person choose such a destiny?

There are many reasons why it happens (and it does, more often than we might guess): religious upbringing could trap such a person in social circles where s/he is required to genuflect at all the right cues, whether s/he agrees with them or not; marriages and families often force an introverted, isolated person to nod and agree with opinions and positions they find loathsome; and many a workplace is populated with some majority that does not hesitate to silence a minority voice, through disapproval, intimidation or ridicule.

What happens in the brain of such a victim?

Passive fear of rejection - The person is afraid of being found out, that their differing views might come to light and leave them ostracized;

Self-doubt – Hopelessly outnumbered, and lacking affirmation and support for their own viewpoint, a natural feeling of doubt may begin to grow;

Intellectual and emotional compromise – A rationalization might seem the way to go, an effort to reconcile how the world feels to the individual with the version of reality that the group insists on promulgating;

Deterioration in cognitive resolve – Under these painful circumstances, it would be hard for such a person (for anyone at all, really) to feel confident in their own powers of reason and evaluation.

That's a pretty sad portrait. But that's how children raised in a religion that seems insane to them often feel; it's how members of politically zealous families must live; it's the harsh destiny of submissive partners in marriage to an emotionally overbearing spouse, and the be-silent-or-be-gone employee.

We can go so far as to say it's a kind of abuse.

What can be done?

It's tempting to conclude that such a black sheep should seek out other black sheep. But even allowing that such liberation is far easier spoken of than accomplished, that is not the answer.

Leaving a cognitive cluster into which one does not fit, only to join a cognitive cluster where one does fit, doesn't solve the ultimate problem: threat of rejection and doubt of self may cease to be factors – but a cognitive cluster, even one that 'feels right,' still leads to intellectual compromise and weak skills in decision-making and problem-solving.

The best of all worlds for any of us, whether we are socially misplaced in our cluster or not, is to cease to be clustered – to seek out and embrace cognitive diversity in all our social participation in the world, wherever possible. Obviously that, too, is easier said than done, but even leaning in the right direction is liberating to the mind and emotions.

And there's one thing further we can do: we can look around us and spot that suppressed person, wherever they might be, and resolve to be safe harbor for them. It doesn't take much – just a few minutes of time listening, authentic interest in that person's thoughts and ideas and point of view; just a few minutes of giving them a brief time to be themselves.

That's not too much to ask of any of us – and to the person who never feels that freedom, even a brief moment of it is Christmas morning...

My ism

When people ask my religion, my answer these days is "Humanism".

I will then get one of several negative responses: "That's not a religion!", "So you think *you're* god?", and so on.

To be sure, I don't really believe that Humanism is a religion, and – oddly – many religious people insist that it is. And, moreover, that my embrace of it is evidence of an innate human need for religion.

I self-identify this way, when asked, simply to avoid the non-word *atheist*, which only makes things worse – it's about everything I *don't* believe, not about what I do. And I'll concede that Humanism does occupy the space in my head that religion once did: it is my private repository for my thoughts and feelings about the same matters of ultimate importance that religions address.

In this sense, perhaps we all do need an 'ism' - a place in our thoughts for maintaining our ideas and convictions about ourselves, our lives, others, life, death, destiny – our feelings about who and what we are.

My own *ism* certainly qualifies. Humanism enshrines my ideas about those things I consider of ultimate importance – that I am part of something much greater than myself; that I am a member of a magnificent group; that there are right ways and wrong ways to live, things we must do and things we must not; and that there are destinies beckoning, for myself and for my kind, that require my best efforts.

Even so, there is a critical difference between my *ism* and all the others. And it's not to do with the non-/existence of deities. Conventional religions (and I'm specifically referencing the patriarchal ones) are tribal in nature. They are social structures, group collectives bound by shared opinion and uniform style of thought. Membership in a religion is contingent upon this uniformity, at least formally. And the priority of this requirement is unassailable, for such groups will shatter almost instantly when dissent creeps into those shared opinions.

But my *ism* has no such requirement. 'Opinion' doesn't enter into it at all. As a Humanist, I simply uphold that all human life is precious, special, bursting with potential, and worthy of protection and nurture. That's it. I don't need my own thoughts reflected back at me in order to remain strong in those convictions.

But there's an even bigger difference, perhaps the most important of all: as a Humanist, I am part of a group that is, by definition, the most all-inclusive of all time. And the membership is all-inclusive by default: all people, everywhere, are members of my tribe, whether they share my beliefs or not; whether they think of themselves that way or not; whether they want to be or not. It is, in my view, the perfect tribe: I get all the benefits of group membership, with none of the drawbacks.

When I enter the world as a Humanist, the dignity of everyone I encounter becomes my priority. Every person's value and worth are enhanced – and the old bromide, 'If everyone is special, then no one is special!' evaporates, because I am no longer elevating individuals in my own biases and preferences, but humankind itself.

When I enter the world as a Humanist, the lethal toxin *Us and Them* dissipates. The very nature of my tribe – *Homo sapiens* – excludes even the possibility of a *Them*. All that space in my brain that I would, in a religion, devote to parsing who is and isn't worthy, who is and isn't acceptable, who is and isn't *like me* is freed up for more important matters.

When I enter the world as a Humanist, I realize I am empowered beyond measure – I am a child of the stars, a member of the elect, the most precious phenomenon in all the universe. Humankind is Nature's ultimate achievement – and I get to be part of it, to enjoy it, to contribute to it. Does this mean I think I am a god? Of course not. *God* is too puny a word for Humankind; we are the universe awakening.

Finally, my *ism* shifts the focus of my life in ways that are not only good for me, but good for everyone I encounter. Its conformities are, by definition, those things which benefit me and others; its possibilities are, in an admittedly religious sense, transcendent – but, again by definition, within reach of human hands.

I'll take my *ism* over all the others, for all these reasons and more; but for one reason in particular - it has made me a better man.

Uncle Scott's Seven Steps

For a stronger intellectual and emotional life, improved decision-making, fuller self-expression and a deeper human experience, Uncle Scott recommends:

1) Stop relying on your cognitive cluster for validation; it exists to throw out false positives;

2) Seek out cognitive diversity;

3) Within cognitive diversity, strive to fully understand your new peers, and to more completely express your own ideas;

4) Allow your thoughts and feelings to be challenged, and respectfully challenge those of others;

5) Make it a recurring practice to self-examine;

6) Defer to whichever leading voice in the group is best suited for the moment, understanding that it will won't always be the same person, and that sometimes it will be you;

7) Within this new environment, seek out and embrace common purpose.

Great reward awaits us all...

Tribalism vs. Globalism

POSIT: The lesson of what is happening to the United States right now - and in other parts of the world, as Authoritarianism casts off its cloak and openly wrestles us all for dominance - is that Humanity has reached its tipping point, with respect to tribalism.

Tribalism and a global humanity are not compatible. There will be one, or there will be the other.

Or there will be nothing.

Kindness is Viral

I sat and talked with my teenage daughter last night. She is my youngest, the baby of the family, and the apple of my eye. As is often the case with lastborns - I, the parent, have already made most of my mistakes, and am close to getting this parenting thing down - our daddy/daughter relationship is warm and trouble-free.

Not so in other relationships. Josie gets along far better with me than she does with her brother and mother. That's to her credit, not mine, but we both acknowledged it, and I thought about it afterwards.

Her mother and brother say that she is at her best around on me (and not them) because I dote on her and think she's still 6 and can't accept that she's almost fully grown.

All of that is perfectly true, of course, but I say it's because kindness is our default. My daughter is always sweet to me. I, in turn, want to treat her with all the kindness in the world.

Kindness begets kindness. When the guy behind the counter at the convenience store says, "Have a great day!", my reflex is to smile and say, "You, too!" When a mother with three kids holds the elevator door for me, I'm inclined to do the same when she and her brood set off. My server at the restaurant offers my kids a couple of desserts that will go to waste if someone doesn't take them - on the house. I tell him I don't need any change when I pay the bill.

The convenience store guy may have a confederate flag on his bumper. The mom-with-kids might believe that gay marriage is an abomination. My server might have voted for Trump. Would I have been so reciprocal with the three of them, had I known these things?

But *I didn't* know those things; the convenience store guy does not look me in the eye and declare, "The South will rise again!" The mom doesn't lean my way and say, "They're putting my marriage at risk!" The server doesn't lean down and whisper, "He's making America great again!" in my ear.

That's just not how the world works. The reality is that most of the people whom we encounter that we don't know and never will are simply Other Human Beings - neither red nor blue, neither straight nor gay, neither faithful nor apostate. Just Other Human Beings. Josie and I know each other as well as family can; these strangers and I are at the opposite end of the intimacy spectrum. Yet here, too, kindness is the default.

And somewhere in the middle, there's the Internet - where we don't begin our encounters with strangers by saying, "Have a great day!", or offering an unsolicited kindness, or taking an interest for its own sake; no, we *lead* with "The South will rise again!" and "Republicans are cruel!" and "Atheists are destroying America!" and "Christian Taliban!"□

On the Internet, we jump straight to the middle. The thing is... There should *be* no middle.

That kindness that we enjoy as our default when we encounter a stranger, that we enjoy many years into a treasured relationship, should persist from Day One, ad infinitum. Can anyone give me a reason why not?

We should be as kind to those we love, many years on, as we are to the guy in the convenience store. Familiarity breeds contempt, the cliché goes, and that's certainly a struggle - but the Internet is making it our default.

I think it's time to move in the other direction. I think Josie and I are getting it right...

If Gods There Be...

If gods there be... we are they.

There is nothing more precious in the universe than a human being. The lowliest child among us is worthy of our deepest respect and our greatest efforts - more valuable than all the world's gold.

Nothing can be more heinous than one human being willfully bringing harm upon another; and no act can be worthier than one human being uplifting another.

We are beginning to see the stars more clearly, now counting planets, and while this exercise thrills the mind as it stirs the intellect, we note that all of these planets – be they hot, cold, big, tiny, dark, light – are empty. The desolation of those worlds makes the life on this one all the more precious.

We are the universe awakening. We are the beginning of life. We are the origin of mind.

If gods there be... we are they.

Bibliography / Recommended Reading

AI in Sci-Fi: Fictional Artificial Minds and the Real World Awaiting Them, Scott Robinson. Paleos Media, 2019

The Children of Babel: Essays on the Inherent Nature of AI and Consciousness, Scott Robinson. Paleos Media, 2018

Godel, Escher, Bach: An Eternal Golden Brain, Douglas Hofstadter. Basic Books, 1999

Homo Deus: A Brief History of Tomorrow, Yuval Noah Harari. Harper Perennial, 2018

I Am a Strange Loop, Douglas Hofstadter. Basic Books, 2008

The Master and His Emissary: The Divided Brain and the Making of the Western World, Iain McGilchrist. Yale University Press, 2019

Mind, Brains, and Science, John Searle. Harvard University Press, 1984

The Second Mountain, David Brooks. Random House, 2019

About the Author

Scott Robinson is a journalist, social scientist, public speaker and musician, and was for 20 years a music critic with the *Louisville Courier-Journal*. He has also been published in *Rolling Stone* and *The Wall Street Journal*. He can be found at **www.facebook.com/scottrobinson99**.